A Treasury of Office Humor

Edited by

Mary E. Hirsch

THE LINCOLN-HERNDON PRESS, INC.
818 South Dirksen Parkway
Springfield, IL 62703

A Treasury of Office Humor

Published by
Lincoln-Herndon Press, Inc.
818 South Dirksen Parkway
Springfield, Illinois 62703
(217) 522-2732

Printed in the United States of America

LIBRARY OF CONGRESS CATALOGUING-IN-PUBLICATION DATA

ISBN 0-942-936-26-4 $10.95
Library of Congress Catalog Card Number 94-078-457
First Printing

This book is dedicated to all my friends who believed in me -- especially Mary S., Mom Mc., Nancy P., Julie R., Judy G., Ellen H., Lori B., Cindy R., Porky, Mary M., Sue A., Cindy S., Geri L., Shelly C., and Jennie S.

It is also dedicated to Wayne, who helped me believe in me.

And for Gabby, who spent hours sitting in my pocket watching me type.

And, finally, it is dedicated to my mom and dad for giving me their humor genes, and to Britta, Perry, and Brett, who are the best part of my world.

A Treasury of Office Humor
by
Mary E. Hirsch

Definitions

Public relations: Telling people what they think of you.

Correction fluid: Pepto Bismol® after a business trip to Mexico.

Embezzle: Good work if you can get it.

Enterprise: Something always being stalked by cling-ons.

Eraser: Text ridder.

Elevators: A raisin' box.

Dynamic organizations: Places where other people work.

Security card: A plastic welcome mat.

Corporate culture: That green stuff growing in the refrigerator.

Door:	The 5 P.M. exit ramp.
Office maintenance:	Janitor in a hum-drum.
Research and development:	Newdist colony.
Vendors:	Sellmates.
Nameplate:	Engraved walnut graffiti.
Marketing:	Corporate target shooting.
Lights:	The only dim thing businesses want.

***

An office worker's nightmare:

Mail Clerk:	"Sir, I need the rest of the day off to attend my grandmother's funeral."
Boss:	"Why certainly. In fact, why don't I go with you."

***

Manager:	"This makes five times this week I've had to reprimand you. What do you have to say for yourself?"
Clerk:	"Thank God it's Friday."

***

Student:	"Do you have any part-time jobs?"
Owner:	"Yes, but right now they are all filled by full-time people."

***

The copier will jam on the past page of a rush project.

Mr. Heffel:	"Ms. Jones, you are always arriving late but leaving exactly at 5:00. What do you have to say for yourself?"
Ms. Jones:	"Well at least I'm partially punctual."

* * *

Sattinger's Law: It works better if you plug it in.
    Arthur Bloch.

* * *

Technology has brought meaning to the lives of many technicians.
    Ed Bluestone.

* * *

Copy service rep:	Dr. Paper.
Copy clerk:	Someone between a Xerox® and a hard place.
Xerox®:	The office clone.
Reproduction:	Repeat performance.

Our Office
Dress
Code:
Cover
your butt
at all
times.

One nice
thing
about my
salary...

No one
will ever
hold me
for
ransom.

**Once I
wanted
total
happiness
but now I
will settle
for a corner
office.**

Copy holder:	That place in the copy machine where your jammed copies are sitting.
Paper supply:	Stacks of bond.
Line to use the copier:	A paper wait.
Copier:	The office wishing machine ("Please let my copies come out; please let my copies come out.").
Copies:	Some 'er reruns.
Copy clerk:	Someone working in the field of reams.
Copier:	Repeat offender.
Copier:	Something that reproduces after it's been fixed.

* * *

MAKING COPIES
(To the tune of "Are You Sleeping?")

This can be sung as a round by all the people waiting in line to use the only copier that is still working.

Making copies, making copies,
Oh what fun, oh what fun,
Put the paper in,
Push the button down,
Watch it run, watch it run.

* * *

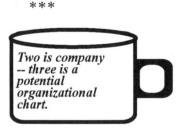

Two is company -- three is a potential organizational chart.

If you forget your resumé in the copier, your supervisor will find it.

Business:	Like burying an elephant — a large undertaking.
Burnout:	What an executive has who would call a subordinate with the same symptoms lazy.
Technology:	What you have to keep up on to keep up on the mortgage.
Business projections:	Prophecy sharing.
Business owners:	People known by the company they keep.
In basket:	Black hole of business.
Office security:	A few video cameras and a guy named Gus.
Office plants:	At times the only signs of life in a company.
Ethics:	Conference table manners.
Conventions:	Tax-deductible vacations.
Cross referencing:	Favorite pasttime of born-again workers.
Disk:	Double-density desk.
Sales:	The sweet sell of success.
Crunch:	When an abundance of work meets a shortage of time.

Cubicle:	A mauve cellblock.
Responsibility:	Corporate fault lines.
Departmentalization:	Organized insanity.
Desk:	A bed with drawers.

***

CEO:	"This budget is late."
Comptroller:	"No it's on time — you just had premature expectations."

***

Vice President:	"Sir, I hate to complain but your son may not be management material."
President:	"What makes you say that?"
Vice President:	"Well, the only way we can get him to read any of our reports or memos is if we include a lot of pictures."

***

Rules are made
to be broken...
down into
policies,
subpolicies,
sub-subpolicies,
etc.

Boss: "I am so tired of having to make one decision after another."

Secretary: "Well maybe I can help. What are you trying to decide on?"

Boss: "Who to blame for my last decision."

* * *

Secretary: "Why do you always answer a question with a question?"

Boss: "Do I?"

* * *

Secretary: "I can't get this done today; I'll finish it tomorrow."

Boss: "If I wanted it tomorrow I would have given it to you tomorrow."

* * *

Your boss will go on vacation the same week another secretary has a family emergency and you will be asked to fill in for her.

COPIER RULES OF LIFE

1. There is never enough paper in the trays to finish your project.
2. The faster you need a copy the longer the line of people waiting to use the copier.
3. When you are copying something personal the boss will stop to chat.
4. When the repair person shows up the problem will disappear.
5. The more urgent the copy, the more likely there will be a paper jam.
6. If an original is irreplaceable it will get jammed in the feeder.
7. The more personal a document, the more likely you will leave it in the copier.
8. No one knows how to change the toner.
9. A new copier is never as good as the one before it, which was worse than the one before that.
10. The more copies you made of a letter, the more likely your boss will change it.

***

Boss: "It's time to clean out our files. Everything that is five years or older should be tossed — but make a copy of it first."

***

Manager to
copier sales rep: "We don't need any more copiers — what we need is a machine you put a piece of paper in and it disappears."

***

THE COPIER'S DOWN

(To the tune of "My Boyfriend's Back")
The only thing in an office that is broke more often than the office staff is the copier.

The copier's down and you're gonna be in trouble,
Hey la, hey la, the thing is down.
Call for service to come here on the double,
Hey la, hey la, the thing is down.
He was here just the other day,
Hey la, hey la, the thing is down.
I don't know why he ever goes away.
Hey la, hey la, the thing is down.

Hey we know it is condemin'
But the copier's a lemon.

It is broke most of the time,
Hey la, hey la, the thing is down.
The damn thing just isn't worth a dime,
Hey la, hey la, the thing is down.
You'll be sorry you came to work,
Hey la, hey la, the thing is down.
'Cause this will make our boss berserk.
Hey la, hey la, the thing is down.

Hey we know it is condemin'
But the copier's a lemon.

What makes you think we'll believe it is fixed,
(Ooooooooooooh, Oooooooooh)
We believed you before but it was just a trick.
(Ooooooooooh, Oooooooooh)
We'll wait and see!

The copier's down and so's your reputation.
Hey la, hey la, the thing is down.
If I were you I'd find a brand new vocation.
Hey la, hey la, the thing is down.

Hey la, hey la, the thing is down.
Hey la, hey la, the thing is down.

* * *

A typo will always be found after you've turned off your computer.

Roses are red,
Violets are blue,
The copier is broken,
So what else is new?

***

Sign above a copier:
"Temporarily In Service."

***

Secretary: "Sir, our copier is a P-I-G-O!"

Office Manager: "Don't you mean a P-I-G?"

Secretary: "No. It's Paper In; Garbage Out ."

***

President:	"It has come to my attention that an estimated 40% of the copies made on our copier have nothing to do with this business."
Vice President:	"That's not so bad."
President:	"Why do you say that?"
Vice President:	"Well, it has come to MY attention that at least 70% of what happens in the office has nothing to do with this business."

* * *

Headquarters:	An edifice complex.
Supplies:	Job benefits that fit nicely in a briefcase, purse or other tote bag.
High productivity:	Doing something really fast no matter how it turns out.
Organizational chart:	A corporate cast of characters.
Petty cash box:	Paltry farm.
Acquisition:	A swell move.
Computers:	The reason men have learned to type.

You can fool some of the people some of the time and some of the people all of the time but you can never live down leaving the restroom with your skirt tucked into your pantyhose.

Computer printer:	A roller ink.
Shredder:	Tale tatter.
I.D. cards:	Stupid looking pictures that have been laminated.
Open system:	Where the doors are removed from the bathroom stalls to discourage lavatory lingering.

* * *

Boss:	"Well how do you like my office? I got $50,000 to decorate it."
Secretary:	"Wow, I never knew you could spend that much money at K-Mart."

***

When designing an office, remember: It's just one short step from the boardroom to the doghouse.

***

I'm essential to the company -- who else would get all the blame

I'm not lazy -- I'm saving all my strength to overthrow management

Lovely to look at, Delightful to touch, But if you try it, I'll sue your fat butt

```
┌─────────────────────────┐
│ If you are not          │
│ confused you            │
│ must be a visitor.      │
└──────┐  ┌──────┐  ┌─────┘
       └──┘      └──┘
```

Plumber:	"Here I am. What's the problem?"
Secretary:	"The president emptied the suggestion box."
Plumber:	"So why do you need me?"
Secretary:	"The toilet got clogged."

* * *

Inez:	"I'm a little nervous about my computer."
Alice:	"Why?"
Inez:	"Today it sent a message demanding a window office."

* * *

When more and more people are thrown out of work
unemployment   results.
Calvin   Coolidge

* * *

Nothing is illegal if one hundred businessmen decide to do it.
Andrew Young

* * *

"Herman, I've reconsidered—I will
marry you!"

A study of economics usually reveals that the best time to buy anything is last year.
      Marty Allen

***

Corporation, n. An ingenious device for obtaining individual profit without individual responsibility.
      Ambrose Bierce, The Devil's Dictionary.

***

Well, I've got just as much conscience as any man in business can afford to keep – just a little, you know, to swear by, as 't were.
      Harriet Beecher Stowe

***

Good for the body is the work of the body, good for the soul is the work of the soul, and good for either, the work of the other.
      Henry David Thoreau

***

Business is the art of extracting money from another man's pocket without resorting to violence.
      Max Amsterdam

***

Business: A great art involving the selling of wind.
      Balastar Gracian

***

A woman's work is never done -- especially if her boss is a man.

Bixley: "Are you happy in your job?"

Martin: "I never knew what real happiness was until I started working here — but then it was too late."

***

Tom: "Do you know what it means to go to an office where you are respected as a human being; where your opinion is sought after and appreciated; where your superiors treat you as an equal?"

Linda: "It means you've gone to the wrong office."

***

Nelson: "This job often puts me between a rock and a hard place."

Henderson: "Why?"

Nelson: "It makes me feel like that fungus no one wants to touch."

***

Paula: "Sorry I'm late."

Paul: "Where have you been all morning?"

Paula: "I was at confession and had to follow a politician. He was in there for over four hours."

***

Mary:	"Welcome back, John. Where did you go on vacation?"
John:	"Europe."
Mary:	"Europe. Wow, you must have a lot of money."
John:	"No, I had a lot of money."

***

OFFICE LIES:

1. It's in the interoffice mail.
2. I have the flu.
3. My aunt (uncle, cousin, mother-in-law) died.
4. I would be happy to stay late.
5. There's nothing I'd rather be doing.
6. That's the funniest joke I've ever heard.
7. I had a flat tire.
8. I baked it myself.
9. My wife (husband) and I have an understanding.
10. I love that tie.
11. "I certify I worked the above listed hours."
12. I'm going to the dentist.
13. You remind me of a movie star but I can't remember which one.
14. I'm almost done with that project.
15. No, I didn't take the last doughnut.

***

OUR COMPANY IS RUN ON TRADITION

(We ran out of new ideas a long time ago)

```
┌─────────────────────────────┐
│ If you can't say            │
│ something nice about        │
│ someone -- please report    │
│ to personnel                │
│ immediately.                │
│                             │
│      ⌐─┐      ⌐─┐           │
└──────┘ └──────┘ └──────────┘
```

Boss: "Why can't you get any work done?"

Secretary: "I just can't seem to get up the ambition to do anything."

Boss: "You know what I do when I don't want to do any work?"

Secretary: "You call a meeting."

        ***

Margie: "Jerry in purchasing told me he has his own lifestyle."

Jennie: "What did you say?"

Margie: "I told him he may have a life but he sure doesn't have style."

        ***

CORRESPONDENCE

1. When a letter has left the office you will find the enclosures on your desk.

2. No letter is so important it can't be lost by the post office.

3. The longer the letter, the more likely it will be deleted from your computer.

4. Envelope glue never tastes good.

5. When you are sending a letter to someone with only initials, if you put Mr. it will be a Ms.; if you put Ms. it will be a Mr.

6. The more important it is that a person not see who the blind copies are going to, the more likely you will forget to take it off the letter.

7. No letter has ever been written that is more important than going to lunch.

8. The more time you have to proof a letter, the less likely you will find a typo.

9. Most letters are dictated within one hour of quitting time; and they all have to go out that day.

10. If a letter is supposed to go to Portland, Oregon, you will send it to Portland, Maine (and vice versa).

* * *

Personnel is very supportive -- like a training bra on Dolly Parton.

HELP...
I'm being held hostage by my paycheck.

I hope I can complete my filing without using bloodshed.

I have so many terrific traits, personnel should be willing to overlook my few unsociable obsessions.

Jerry:	"I saw the eclipse of the moon last night — it totally disappeared."
Sherry:	"Oh sure, when the moon disappears it's an eclipse; when I disappear it's goofing off."

***

Henry:	"I thought I was going to have some extra money this paycheck."
Henrietta:	"What happened?"
Henry:	"Cindy in Accounting is getting married so there goes that dollar."

***

"The horror of that moment," the King went on, "I shall never, never forget!"

"You will, though," the Queen said, "if you don't make a memorandum of it."

Lewis Carroll

***

Why is a prayer shorter than a department meeting?
God listens.

***

I have received memos so swollen with managerial babble that they struck me as the literary equivalent of assault with a deadly weapon.

Peter Baida

***

I'll never get fired -- I have a lousy parking spot and an office with no window.

The only way to find out if a memo or a report is unnecessary is to read the darn thing — which could turn out to be a waste of time.
Supervisor's Bulletin, 10/30/85, No. 744

* * *

A memorandum is written not to inform the reader but to protect the writer.
Dean Acheson

* * *

A conference is a gathering of important people who, singly, can do nothing but together can decide that nothing can be done.
Fred Allen

* * *

There is no better place in the world to find out the shortcomings of each other than a conference.
Will Rogers

* * *

Never dump a good idea on a conference table. It will belong to the conference.
Jane Trahey

* * *

A committee is a thing that takes a week to do what one good man can do in an hour.
Elbert Hubbard

.... or a woman has already done, but no one noticed.
Mary Hirsch

***

Outside of traffic, there is nothing that has held this country back as much as committees.
Will Rogers

***

In a small company, one person's hunch can be enough to launch a new product. In a big company, the same concept is likely to be buried in committees for months.
Al Ries and Jack Trout

***

The less you enjoy serving on committees, the more likely you are to be pressured to do so.
Charles Issawi

***

The usefulness of a meeting is in inverse proportion to the attendance.
Lane Kirkland

***

If you can't say something nice
--
you have management potential.

"I'M BETWEEN JOBS. MY COMPANY MOVED AND THEY DIDN'T TELL ME WHERE THEY WENT."

When you become too senior to work, then your work is going to meetings.
Woodrow H. Sears, Jr.

***

Try skipping a meeting if you want to find out how important it is.
Robert Townsend

***

CEO: "This party is sure dull. I think I'll go home."

Mail Clerk: "Well, that should liven things up considerably."

***

Tom: "Why are you golfing instead of working?"

Tim: "I have the flu."

***

Secretary: "Wasn't the Christmas party fun?"

Boss: "I wasn't there. I had a flat tire and missed it."

Secretary: "No wonder everyone said it was the best party ever."

***

Employee 1: "Why aren't you having anything to drink?"

Employee 2: "Who wants to risk seeing two of our boss?"

***

Bill:	"I've found a great way to start the day."
Jill:	"How?"
Bill:	"I go right back to bed."

* * *

Nan:	"Bob in Sales has all kinds of money."
Jane:	"Is he rich?"
Nan:	"No, he's a coin collector."

* * *

Terry:	"Come quick!
Larry:	"What's wrong?"
Terry:	"There's something strange on my plant."
Larry:	"What is it?"
Terry:	"A leaf."

* * *

Hank:	"Where are you going for vacation this year?"
Hillary:	"To the bank for a loan."

* * *

| Bill: | "Come on, John, get into the football pool. It's only $3.00. What have you got to lose?" |
| John: | "Sure, that's what they said about my marriage license." |

***

BORN TO BE DIALED
(To the tune of "Born to Be Wild")

In most offices a receptionist is expected to be a cross between Kim Basinger, Mother Theresa, and Aunt Bea.

Get the coffee brewin',
Open up the office,
Primping in the bathroom,
So the public will adore us.

Picking up the phone lines,
Trying to take a message,
From some guy who's talking,
While chewing on his breakfast.

Yes sir I can take the pressure,
And do my work in a cheerful way,
Maintain our corporate image,
Come what may.

'Cause like a true office child,
I was born,
Born to be dialed,
While others might cry,
I never blink an eye.

***

Office Manager:	"You're late. Don't you know what time we start working here?"
Miller:	"No sir. Every day when I get here everyone is already working."

***

Boss:	"Is there any excuse for this sloppy work?"
Hanson:	"No, but give me a few minutes and I'll come up with one."

***

Betty:	"You can always tell when Bill is having trouble at home."
Larry:	"How?"
Betty:	"He comes in on time."

***

Boss:	"Why didn't you call and tell us you wouldn't be in?"
Clerk:	"I couldn't find my cordless phone."

***

Jack:	"I demand to be paid what I'm worth!"
Boss:	"We can't do that."
Jack:	"Why not?"
Boss:	"There are minimum wage laws we have to obey."

***

What the rest of the office does while you are in a meeting

1. Eat the doughnuts they told you didn't show up.

2. Hook all your paper clips together and then put them back in your desk.

3. Write personal letters.

4. Look through Victoria's Secret catalogs.

5. Over-water your plants.

6. Make long-distance calls to their friends and family from your phone.

7. Read your E-mail messages.

8. Register your house as a Bed & Breakfast.

9. Practice the tubas they are hiding under their desks.

10. Catch up on their sleep after a rough weekend.

* * *

PLEEEEEEEEZ... I'm too busy to kid around. When do you really want it?

Man
Proposes

God
Disposes

Manage-
ment
Imposes.

Most of
my work
can be
done
better if
I'm not
fully
conscious.

**My career
is right on
track with
a speeding
locomotive
headed
towards me.**

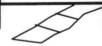

Typewriter:	Prehistoric keyboard.
Mergers:	Corporate copulation.
Norm:	The guy who fixes your chair when it squeaks.
Normative:	A relative of Norm's.
ASAP:	A situation generally caused by someone else's Advanced Slowness And Procrastination.
Leaving early:	Premature evacuation.
Wastebasket:	Rubble shooter.
Lap top computer:	Crotchword puzzles.
Revenue:	When it pays to be gross.

* * *

Discussing his poor performance in the last year the stock clerk said, "When there is something important to get done my brain says, 'Quick, think of all the different options.' Then my heart says, 'Start pumping adrenalin so you can move quickly.' Then my feet say, 'Move quickly to the place you need to be.'"

"So why don't you do these things?" asked the personnel administrator.

"Because just when I'm going to, my body says 'Who, me??????'"

* * *

CEO:	"Well, the results are back from your aptitude tests."
VP:	"Great, what kind of work am I suited for?"
CEO:	"Unemployment."

* * *

> **There's no excuse for sloppy work -- but there is a committee looking into it.**

Fred: "I'm going to go to business school."

Frank: "Why?"

Fred: "So I'll be out of a better job."

                    * * *

Boss: "Why are you always late?"

Stock room clerk: "I never get up in time."

Boss: "Set your alarm clock earlier."

Stock room clerk: "I don't have an alarm clock."

Boss: "Why not?"

Stock room clerk: "It scares the daylight out of me."

                    * * *

Meetings:	Time wasted around a piece of walnut wood.
Department Meeting:	People operating under the delusion that things change if you talk about them.
Mailroom:	A sorted place.
Memo writer:	Someone whose word is never done.
Memos:	BS with a distribution list.
Directive:	A non-secular commandment.
Mail cart:	The little read wagon.
Records clerk:	Someone who heard the call of the file.
Documents:	Pieces of paper that as soon as you throw them away someone will want to have.

* * *

Secretary:	"I think we should consider getting a new coffee machine."
Office Manager:	"Why, the one we have is just fine."
Secretary:	"Well I just heard that Dr. Kavorkian has asked for our coffee recipe."

* * *

Boss:	"Mr. Jones, you should have been here at 8:30."
Mr. Jones:	"Why, what happened?"

* * *

Personnel:	"Bill, you can't give your manager the finger — it has upset him."
Bill:	"Well it wouldn't have upset him if he hadn't turned around."

***

Boss (on phone):	"You sound really sick with that cough."
Employee:	"I should — I practiced all night."

***

Boss:	"Now that you are with us are you happy?"
New Employee:	"Yes, I certainly am."
Boss:	"What were you before you started here?"
New Employee:	"Much happier."

***

Doodling:	Taking thorough notes at important meetings.
Dictionary:	The last place in the world you look for just the right word.
Intercom:	A beg-n-call.
Overnight delivery:	The procrastinator's best friend.
Forms:	A waste of time — in triplicate.
Form letter:	Correspondence that says nothing — but says it very politely.
Files:	Coffee mug coasters.

Humor in the workplace:	What management thinks is a good idea as long as it isn't used.
Kudos:	A corporate line of credit.
Input:	Failing to stop at an interjection.
It's on hold":	Business jargon for what your mother meant when she said "We'll see."
Office manual:	CrEdO.
Jargon:	More slang for the buck.
File room:	The center of retention.
File folder:	A manila wastebasket.

***

Johnson:	"How can you fire me? When I was hired you said this was the most secure job in the company."
Personnel:	"The job is secure — but you aren't."

***

What you don't know won't hurt you -- but at a meeting always pretend you know it anyways.

"I'M ON MY COFFEE BREAK RIGHT NOW, HUGO. I'LL CALL YOU BACK DURING WORKING HOURS."

Interviewer:	"This job requires someone who is very responsible."
Applicant:	"That's me. At my last seven jobs, whenever anything went wrong, I was responsible."

* * *

Sherry:	"Why are you packing up your things?"
Mary:	"My boss said something so terrible I won't come back until he apologizes."
Sherry:	"What did he say?"
Mary:	"You're fired."

* * *

Manager:	"I want you to fire my secretary."
Personnel:	"Why?"
Manager:	"She is getting careless about her appearance."
Personnel:	"We can't fire someone for not being good looking."
Manager:	"She's great looking — she just never appears at work."

* * *

Applicant:	"Can you tell me what this job is really like?"
Interviewer:	"Well it would be best if you thought of this job as a hot dog — you're better off not knowing everything about it."

* * *

The perfect job comes along once in a lifetime but until then I'm stuck here.

Interviewer:	"What kind of hours do you want to work?"
Applicant:	"Noon to one, with an hour for lunch."

***

Applicant:	"Does this company have any death benefits?"
Interviewer:	"Yes it does. When you die you don't have to come to work anymore."

***

Interviewer:	"We treat our employees just like family."
Applicant:	"Gee, don't you want us to stay with the company?"

***

Boss:	"If you want to continue working here you will have to start coming in bright and early."
Johnson:	"How about one out of two?"

***

Clerk:	"The company president must think of me as a fine wine."
Clerk 2:	"Why?"
Clerk:	"He puts me in the cellar."

***

A very handsome janitor met a beautiful woman at a bar.
"What do you do for a living?" the janitor asked.
"I'm a corporate attorney for a Fortune 500 company," the woman replied. "And what about you?"
"I'm a CEO at Acme Enterprises," the janitor bragged.
They spent the rest of the evening talking, really hit it off and began to see each other on a regular basis. One day the attorney decided to surprise her new lover at work. When she showed up she found him vacuuming the hall.
"I thought you said you were a CEO!" she shouted at him.
"I am," he replied, "I am the Cleaner of Every Office."

***

Executive Review:	The muddle between the beginning and end of a project.
Excuse:	An explanation why a mistake is really someone else's fault.
Miscellaneous File:	A stopover on the way to the wastebasket.
Envelopes:	Desk-top stuffing.
Logo:	Corporate tatoo.
Post-Its®:	Gummy bearers.
Phone:	Workus interruptus.
Fax:	Quick writ.

Facsimile operator:	Keeps up with the fax of life.
Facsimile:	A Fax in a tuxedo.
E-mail:	Computerized manure spreader.
Memos:	Heat-seeking epistles.
Company policy:	A joke with no punchline.
Company manual:	Hot air in a three-ring binder.
Breakfast meeting:	Something everyone is too late arriving at for anything to get accomplished.
Successful committee:	A group of four managers — three of whom are consistently absent.
Conference room:	Where you can rendezvous with a view.
Brainstorming:	In most organizations a light mist at best.
Agenda:	A written list of things a committee probably won't accomplish.
Audio-visual aids:	Something that makes boring graphics easier to see.
Decision maker:	Someone who does not serve on a committee.
Roundtable:	Where an idea is surrounded and forced to give up.
Correspondence file:	Compose heap.
Agenda:	Brainstorming with Roman numerals.
Rules:	A performance command.

* * *

Boss:	"Why are you always late?"
Worker:	"I'm having problems with my legs."
Boss:	"Varicose veins? Pulled hamstring? Water on the knee?"
Worker:	"No, they just don't want to get out of bed in the morning."

* * *

Clerk:	"I begin every morning with a prayer."
Boss:	"That is quite admirable. What do you pray for?"
Clerk:	"I pray it is Saturday and I can go back to sleep."

* * *

Employee:	"Why is that clock always fast?"
Boss:	"Well, something in the company has to be!"

* * *

**My job involves TLC:
T aking
L ots of
C rap**

"Of course I sent that fax. I mailed it myself."

LEADER OF THE FAX (To the tune of "Leader of the Pack")
Office romances almost always end in tragedy!!

Is that Jimmy's corporate ID badge you're wearing?
Um, hummmm.
Where'd you meet him?

I met him in the coffee room,
He turned around and smiled at me,
Get the picture?
(Yes we see.)
That's when I fell for,
The Leader of the Fax.

My boss was always putting him down,
(DOWN   DOWN)
She said he didn't know a verb from a noun,
(DIDN'T KNOW A VERB FROM A NOUN)
She said our love was doomed,
'Cause he worked in the mailroom,
That I'd never be promoted,
With the Leader of the Fax.

My supervisor said find someone new,
I had to tell my Jimmy we're through,
He stopped faxing and asked me why,
I said "'cause you don't own a tie,"
I'm sorry if I hurt you,
The Leader of the Fax.

As he ran away down that office hall,
I begged him not to go blabbin' it,
But he never had the chance at all,
'Cause he was crushed by a falling file cabinet.

LOOK OUT, LOOK OUT, LOOK OUT!

I felt so helpless what could I say,
Seeing him flattened out that way,
At work I always look so grimly,
Everytime I receive a facsimile,
I'll never forget you
The Leader of the Fax.

***

Commuter on a crowded bus:	"How many people does this bus carry comfortably?"
Driver:	"None."

***

Interviewer:	"Are you married?"
Applicant:	"No."
Interviewer:	"Why not?"
Applicant:	"I'm in no hurry."
Interviewer:	"Then, I guess you are management material."

***

Interviewer:	"How long did you work at your last job?"
Applicant:	"Thirty years."
Interviewer:	"But you are only 25. How could you have worked there 30 years?"
Applicant:	"A lot of overtime."

***

> I never knew what happiness was until I took this job...
> now it's too late.

Employee:	"I'm afraid if I don't get a raise I will have to start thinking about moving on."
Boss:	"Can I get you the number of a moving company?"

***

Interviewer:	"Are you a yes-man?"
Applicant:	"Maybe."

***

Owner:	"Boy, do I have a big problem."
Manager:	"What is it?"
Owner:	"I have a part-time job opening."
Manager:	"So what's the problem?"
Owner:	"I have three nephews and two nieces."

***

Personnel:	"How fast do you type?"
Applicant:	"Who's watching?"

***

Personnel Director:	"I'm sorry but we are going to have to let you go."
Bayers:	"But I know my job backwards."
Personnel Director:	"That is the problem."

***

Interviewer: "Why were you fired from your last job?"

Applicant: "Well I worked for the Animal Rights Council and
                      they caught me slapping a mosquito."

* * *

I like work; it fascinates me. I can sit and look at it for hours. I love to
keep it by me; the idea of getting rid of it nearly breaks my heart.
        Jerome K. Jerome

* * *

What's not worth doing is not worth doing well.
        Don Hebb

* * *

Labor, n. One of the processes by which A acquires property for B.
        Ambrose Bierce

* * *

It is not necessary that a man should earn his living by the sweat of his
brow, unless he sweats easier than I do.
        Henry David Thoreau

* * *

Work: Drudgery in disguise.
        Anonymous

* * *

Work is the province of cattle.
        Dorothy Parker

* * *

The brain is a wonderful organ; it starts working the moment you get up in the morning and does not stop until you get into the office.
Robert Frost

***

Work is accomplished by those employees who have not yet reached their level of incompetence.
Laurence J. Peter

***

One cannot walk through a mass production factory and not feel that one is in Hell.
W. H. Auden

***

Sometimes I worry about being a success in a mediocre world.
Lily Tomlin

***

Opportunities are usually disguised as hard work, so most people don't recognize them.
Ann Landers

***

Don't start anything you can't fin...

TGIP Thank God It's Payday.	The world is coming to an end.... so why do your filing?	Success is the best revenge -- but an unordered pizza delivered at 2 in the morning can tide you over until success arrives.

Ms. Fraser: "I've decided to quit."

Mr. Stern: "Why?"

Ms. Fraser: "There's nothing left that I want to steal."

                        * * *

Applicant: "Can you give me a job?"

Interviewer: "I'm sorry but we have more employees than we need
                    already."

Applicant: "That's okay — the little bit of work I would do will
                    never be noticed."

                        * * *

Interviewer: "Are you enthusiastic?"

Applicant: "I'm fired with enthusiasm — each and every time."

                        * * *

Boss: "If you do good work we will give you a raise."

Applicant: "I knew there would be catch to it."

                        * * *

Interviewer: "Do you have any special talents?"

Applicant: "Everyday I do the New York Times crossword puzzle
                    in ink."

Interviewer: "That's great, but I was thinking of something
                    related to your job."

Applicant: "So was I."

                        * * *

Interviewer:	"I hope you don't mind me asking all these questions."
Applicant:	"No, I have a six-year-old at home."

$*\,*\,*$

Applicant:	"Is the death rate any higher in this job?"
Interviewer:	"No — it's one to a person."

$*\,*\,*$

Applicant:	"How much do you pay?"
Interviewer:	"$6.00 an hour for the next first six months, then $7.50 an hour after that. Do you want the job?"
Applicant:	"Sure. I'll be back in six months."

$*\,*\,*$

Interviewer:	"You are asking for a very high salary for someone with no experience."
Applicant:	"Yes, but I'm going to have to work even harder to look busy."

$*\,*\,*$

Messenger	Will give you a run for his money.
Word processing:	A department with all types in it.
Menial tasks:	Work that is usually preceded with the words. "In your spare time..."

> There is nothing I wouldn't do to advance my career except come in early, stay late, work harder, and be a productive member of society.

Exchange of ideas:	When you tell your supervisor your idea and then it becomes his idea.
Work:	A deep sleep spoiled.
Behavioral processes:	Actions that are done in direct proportion to who is in the area.
Clock watching:	Doing time.
Workaholics:	Anyone who puts in more hours than you do.
Adaptive subsystems:	How you do the job when no one from the system is around.
Time study:	Watching the clock until it's time to go home.
Bus:	A working class limo.
Clerk:	Designated flunky.
Support staff:	The people sitting downwind when the shit hits the fan.
Flunky:	A do-minion.
Stockroom clerk:	A poet waiting to be discovered.

***

SCHWADRON

"MINISKIRTS ARE MAKING A COMEBACK, SO I FIGURED WHAT THE HECK! WHAT DO YOU THINK, MISS WAYNE?"

Clerk 1:	"They hired a new supervisor for us. I know he is going to be terrible to work for."
Clerk 2:	"How do you know that? You haven't even met him yet."
Clerk 1:	"Well I heard his last job was as a federal maximum security prison warden."
Clerk 2:	"Well that doesn't mean anything."
Clerk 1:	"Oh yeah! He calls this job a lateral career move."

* * *

Manager:	"Why do you have a picture of Jimmy Hoffa on your desk?"
Clerk:	"He's a role model for me in my job."
Manager:	"Because he was head of the Teamsters?"
Clerk:	"No. Because he can disappear without anyone finding him."

* * *

Office Manager:	"Ms. Adams, we have 150 employees here and 149 of them are on time every day. Why aren't you?"
Ms. Adams:	"Well if they didn't hog all the elevators I'd be here too."

* * *

Company line:	Brainwashing with a logo on the soap.
Conference:	Where many bodies meet but few minds do.
Breakdown in corporate communications:	Slow 'n tell.
Conference call:	A bunch of phonees and one phoner.
Board meeting:	A barbershop without the barber.
Cellular phone:	How an executive can play golf and be sick in bed at the same time.
Spelling:	Ah reel empourtent zkil two haf.
Communications:	Corporate contact sports.
Buzzwords:	Social-climbing disease.
Calendar:	Where appointments stay at the Pencil Inn.
Call in sick:	What you do before you clear your throat in the morning.
Task force:	A body of people who are "looking into it."
Suggestion box:	The bathroom wall of corporate America.
Bureaucracy:	A game you can win only by crossing the red tape.
Committee:	A group of people who take on a task no one person in their right mind would do.
Tickler file:	Corporate masturbation of the memory.

* * *

The Prayer of One About to Have a Review:

Oh grant me such a great big raise,
So big that even I,
When filing next year's income tax,
Won't feel compelled to lie.

* * *

Manager: "So what is the new guy like?"

Supervisor: "He is nice, generous, funny, and efficient."

Manager: "Oh, that's why no one likes him."

* * *

President: "So what do you think of the new department manager?"

VP: "She is warm, intelligent, efficient, responsible — and she definitely has your eyes."

* * *

Boss: "How long will it take you to finish this project?"

Assistant: "When do you have to have it?"

Boss: "I need it by Wednesday morning.

Assistant: "What a coincidence......"

* * *

CHURN, CHURN, CHURN
(To the tune of "Turn, Turn, Turn")

NEVER be so efficient or organized that you are caught up with your work. If anyone finds out they will not assume you are an exceptional employee — they will assume you do not have enough to do and will rectify that immediately.

Here everyday,
Churn, churn, churn,
There'll be no shirking,
Churn, churn, churn,
'Cause it's time for us to be working.

A time to get up,
A time to sit down,
A time to type,
A time to file,
A time to run,
A time to wait,
A time for lunch,
Oh...I guess it's too late.

Here everyday,
Churn, churn, churn,
There'll be no shirking,
Churn, churn, churn,
'Cause it's time for us to be working.

* * *

"I have a dream job" said one accountant.

"How you must dread going to bed!" said the other.

* * *

New manager: "What is the name of the company president?"

Old manager: "Ms. Peterson."

New manager: "How will I recognize her?"

Old manager: "Well if you see two people talking and one looks
                 terribly bored, the other is Peterson."

***

When I have a tough job in the plant and can't find an easy way to do it, I
have a lazy man put on it. He'll find an easy way to do it in ten days.
Then we adopt that method.
    Clarence E. Bleicher

***

Like every man of sense and good feeling, I abominate work.
    Aldous Huxley

***

Work is the refuge of people who have nothing better to do.
    Oscar Wilde

***

Anyone can do any amount of work provided it isn't the work he is
supposed to be doing at that moment.
    Robert Benchley

***

I've met a few people in my time who were enthusiastic about hard work.
And it was just my luck that all of them happened to be men I was
working for at the time.
    Bill Gold

***

Work: Exercise continued to fatigue.
      Samuel Johnson

* * *

Work: What you do so that some time you won't have to do it anymore.
      Alfred Polgar

* * *

Interviewer: "It seems to me that you have had a lot of jobs in the past. How do I know you won't quit this job?"

Applicant: "I never quit a job. I always stay until I'm fired."

* * *

Human Resources
Director: "Well what do you think of Mr. Jones?"

Department
Manager: "He might be a little old for the job."

Human Resources
Director: "Why?"

Department
Manager: "He listed his first job as cabin boy for Columbus."

* * *

Owner: "What can you do?"

Applicant: "Nothing."

Owner: "Oh, I already have a vice president to do that."

* * *

Boss:	"Mr. Jones, I don't know how we'd get along without you."
Jones:	"Thank you, sir."
Boss:	"...but we are going to try."

***

Supervisor:	"Normally I don't do this, but I'm going to mix business with pleasure."
Boss:	"Oh, how?"
Supervisor:	"I quit!"

***

Interviewer:	"What was your last job?"
Applicant:	"Plant manager."
Interviewer:	"Really, what did that entail?"
Applicant:	"I watered 'em twice a week."

***

Interviewer:	"What kind of skills do you have?"
Applicant:	"Well I can erase 50 words per minute."

***

There are an enormous number of managers who have retired on the job.
        Peter Drucker

***

If you split the seams of your shorts at the company picnic no one will tell you until Monday morning.

Steady Job: A rocking chair — it keeps you busy, but you don't get anywhere.
>Leonard Levinson

* * *

No man does as much today as he is going to do tomorrow.
>Bob Edwards

* * *

Work is the greatest thing in the world, so we should always save some of it for tomorrow.
>Don Herold

* * *

What is worth doing is worth the trouble of asking somebody to do it.
>Ambrose Bierce

* * *

Dear Miss Manners: As a businessman, how do I allow a businesswoman to pay for my lunch?
Miss Manners: With credit card or cash, as she prefers.
>Judith Martin

* * *

Work expands so as to fill the time available for its completion.
C. Northcote Parkinson

***

Planning:
Something managers spend a lot of time doing so that their work piles up and then all of a sudden it has to be done right away — by someone else.

Power base:
Core.

Power lunch:
Where only the talk is cheap.

Travel:
What everyone loved to do until they had to do it for work.

Accounting:
Where it's better not to have anything lie in the balance.

Department:
A group of people all involved in not doing the same thing.

Department heads:
The individuals who mistakenly believe they are in charge.

Dictating:
What Hitler did and management does.

Decision making:
Shoveling air.

Cutbacks:
Bargain basement back stabbers.

Corporate loyalty:
That burning sense that someone is watching you.

If you can't delegate, at least mumble.

"What's the minimum level of competence here?"

Cost cutter:	Someone with no taste for accounting.
Creativity:	A word commonly used in a job description, often found on a resumé, and seldom seen in action.
Do lunch:	A meal where you prefer your company to the company.

* * *

Going to work for a large company is like getting on a train. Are you going sixty miles an hour, or is the train going sixty miles an hour and you're just sitting still?
> J. Paul Getty

* * *

Some men are born mediocre, some men achieve mediocrity, and some men have mediocrity thrust upon them.
> Joseph Heller

* * *

Be awful nice to 'em going up, because you're gonna meet 'em all comin' down.
> Jimmy Durante

* * *

Life is a series of yellow pads.
> George Stevens

* * *

Man cannot live by incompetence alone.
> Laurence Peter

* * *

Manager:	"Whatever made you put this paragraph in your memo?"
Assistant:	"I copied it from the company president's monthly report."
Manager:	"And an excellent paragraph it is."

* * *

A manager had agreed to meet the company president for tennis at 6 a.m. the next morning. Not being much of a morning person she said, "In case I'm a little late, go ahead and beat me."

* * *

New employee:	"Is it true the boss won't stop you and give you work if you are carrying a file?"
Old timer:	"It depends on how fast you carry it."

* * *

There are three kinds of employees: those who make things happen; those who watch things happen; and those who have no idea at all what is happening.

* * *

Garrison:	"Mr. Jones has the cleanest mind in the office."
Harrison:	"Why do you say that?"
Garrison:	"Well look how often he changes it."

* * *

Linhoff:	"How was your vacation?"
Weber:	"Great, but it sure is nice to be back at work."
Linhoff:	"Why?"
Weber:	"I need the rest."

***

Controller:	"Folks, we are having a budget crunch and everyone is going to have to help in order to pull the company through."
Manager:	"Well, name one way we can help."
Controller:	"To start with from now on when you want something from the boss you will have to margarine him up."

***

Appointment:	Chance to get away from your desk.
Appointment book:	What you must have to play the dating game.
Aide:	An administrative assistant who gets paid minimum wage.
Ambition:	What you have when you start a job.

> Don't worry about tomorrow -- Everythin will turn out completel screwed-up.

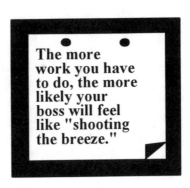

The more work you have to do, the more likely your boss will feel like "shooting the breeze."

Blame:	Blunder-wear.
Bookkeeper:	Poorly paid accountant.
Busywork:	What fills in those long hours between commuting.
Classical management:	Where the Bach is passed.
Closed system:	Constipation administration.
Business cards:	What grown-ups trade instead of baseball cards.
Brown noser:	Someone who would guard the door while his boss made love to his wife
Branch office:	Where you say you are when you are going to play golf.
Briefcase:	A male purse.
Help:	Something you brag about giving and deny ever needing.
Delegating:	Putting work on someone else's desk when they aren't looking.
Interfacing:	When two people with briefcases talk.

Indecision:	Management's final word.
Accountant:	A fortune bookie.
Inferior:	Being afraid of your in-box.
Long-term project:	Corporate punishment.
Junior executive:	Corporate serfer.
Image:	Grown-up dress-up.
Management by objectives:	Goal intending.
Management:	Reigning inside.
Managerial team:	A corporate Please Squad.
Manager:	The person who makes sure everything gets done on time, that things runs smoothly, and who brings the donuts to the weekly meetings.
Hobbies:	Work you do at home.

* * *

Have you ever had a feeling you think your career is on hold when it's really been disconnected?

* * *

Resist temptation -- but give in to the boss's kid selling Girl Scout cookies

> **People here are always learning from their mistakes -- and hopefully they won't do the same thing at their next job.**

Manager:	"Well it's taken almost a year but my department is finally functioning as a team."
Owner:	"How did you do that?"
Manager:	"The entire department is against me."

***

President:	"Well you've been here three months. What have you accomplished?"
New employee:	"To be honest, absolutely nothing. I spend most of my day shuffling papers, reading memos I don't understand, and looking busy. In fact I'm not sure anyone even knows I'm here."
President:	"Well I'm going to make you a vice president, move you into a beautiful office suite, and raise your salary to $100,000 annually."
New employee:	"Gee thanks."
Company President:	"Is that all you have to say?"
New employee:	"Gee thanks, Mom!"

***

Manager:	"I wanted to let you know that I'm pregnant."
VP of Personnel:	"Will you be working after the baby is born?"
Manager:	"Oh no, I want to keep this job."

***

CEO:	"Are you scared about your first day on the job?"
Jr. Executive:	"No, it's the last day I'm scared about."

***

Boss:	"She is very tactful."
Manager:	"I guess she must know just what to say and when to say it."
Boss:	"No. She knows when to shut up."

***

Nothing lasts forever except the day before you start your vacation.

I seem to
have
misplaced
my key to
success.

I like
People
so I try
to
leave
them
alone.

I must be
dying --
my boss
just gave
me a
compliment.

Quality control:	Making sure nobody's work is so good that it raises the level of expectation.
Work group:	An execution squad that is often shooting blanks.
Schedule:	A written plan to let people know just how far behind they are running.
Networking:	People helping people as long as they can share the credit and pass the blame.
Procrastination:	Ongoing wait gain.
Quality Control Dept.:	A Guaran-tee Party.
Weekend:	Two more working days until Monday.
Seminars:	A day off of work, with pay and a notebook.
Power suit:	A well-tailored dark suit worn over a pair of blue leotards with a red "S" on the chest.
Team building:	Managerial method to pawn off his or her work.
Sucking up:	Posterior postulating.
Teamwork:	A group of people taking credit for the work of one person.
Teamwork:	How a mutiny gets started.
Opportunity:	What knocks on your office door when you're down the hall getting coffee.
Team spirit:	Being willing to just say yes.
Supervisor:	A watch power.

Out basket:	A you-clearer waste dump.
Parking spot:	When your job status is between the lines.
Office manager:	A bossetary.
Spreadsheet:	Someone who gives their sheet to everyone else to do.
Title:	Put on a business card to make a listing impression.
Prioritizing:	Paper shuffling with a purpose.
Procedures:	The road Les travelled and Donna travelled and Karen travelled and Bob travelled....
Training groups:	Thom McCann boot camp.
Principles of management:	Let's make an ideal.
Overtime:	When you do the work that didn't get done because you were doing the work that had to be done.

***

I am not an ass-kisser...

I like to wash my boss's car and do his laundry -- on a rock by the river.

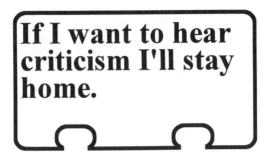

If I want to hear criticism I'll stay home.

IN-BOX
(To the tune of "Annie's Song")

Apparently executives believe that a manager's "In-Box" is a magical place where work can be put and magically gets done! This song is dedicated to all of us Houdinis.

You fill up my in-box,
Till it's overflowing,
With your notes and your letters,
And your memos and thoughts,
With "do this" and "find this"
And "get me a copy."
You fill up my in-box,
Again and again.

Cut me some slack, please,
Let me take a short breather,
Let me go to the bathroom,
Let me put down the phone,
Let me water my ivy,
Let me finish my sandwich,
Cut me some slack, please,
Just leave me alone.

***

If you can't respect me at least pity me.

I'll be glad when the day is over and I can take my ass out of the sling.

It would help in tackling my job if I knew the location of its weakest points.

TILL THERE WAS ME (To the tune of "Till There Was You")

For bookkeepers everywhere who have to keep companies solvent —
whether or not there is any income.

There were bills on your desk,
But you never paid them timely,
No you never paid them at all,
Till there was me.

There were loans on your books,
But your rates were never prime, see,
No your rates were not prime at all,
Till there was me.

And there was payroll,
And quarterly taxes, they tell me,
Your insurance premiums
Were all overdue.

There was cash all around,
But you never saved a dime, see,
No you never saved it at all,
Till there was me.

***

Jenkins:	"Have you ever gotten lost in your work?"
Wilson:	"No, but I am bewildered quite often."

***

Personnel :	"I don't know how to break this to you."
Supervisor:	"What is it?"
Personnel :	"Well, let me put it this way — you are giving dull a bad name."

***

***

A boorish junior executive asked a co-worker what type of apology he should make to the president of the company for missing his party. "Oh don't worry, Bob," replied the co-worker, "say nothing. You weren't missed."

***

Funeral services were being held for a department manager who had been disliked by everyone in the company. He was always critical, yelling at everyone, and just plain nasty. On the day of the funeral the sun was shining but by the time the service was over the sky had turned gray. All of a sudden there was a bright bolt of lightning followed by a loud clap of thunder. "Well, I guess he got there!" said his secretary.

***

They once painted a picture of the company's supervisors at work — it was a still life.

***

The department managers disbanded the company choir before it started. They discovered there could be only one director.

***

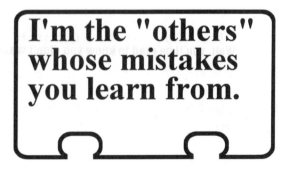

I'm the "others" whose mistakes you learn from.

Betty:	"Doesn't your husband get mad when you work so late?"
Barb:	"I don't have a husband."
Betty:	"Then why are you working late?"

* * *

Personnel Mgr:	"Your department complains that you are too impersonal."
Dept. Mgr:	"Me? Impersonal? Who said that? I'll bet it was Badge 4768435, wasn't it?"

* * *

Jenkins:	"Why was Johnson promoted?"
Boss:	"He came up with a great new product idea."
Jenkins:	"What was it?"
Boss:	"A coffin with a lifetime guarantee."

* * *

Manager:	"Remember all the worrying you did about your report?"
Jr. Executive:	"Yes."
Manager:	"Well, you'll be glad to know you didn't waste your time."

* * *

Lester: "My boss and I have many differences of opinion."

Leslie: "Really, does it cause any problems?"

Lester: "No. She doesn't know it."

* * *

Boss: "I'm worried about this big deal."

Assistant: "What can I do to help?"

Boss: "Bite my nails for me."

* * *

Boss: "Why are you asking for a second computer?"

Manager: "I am making so many mistakes I can't keep
                   blaming it on the same computer."

* * *

I am the captain of my soul;
I rule it with stern joy;
And yet I think I had more fun,
When I was cabin boy.
            Keith Preston

* * *

The president of our company says he's surrounded by yes
men. He told me so himself, and I agreed with him.
            Anonymous

* * *

Sharks have been swimming the oceans unchallenged for thousands of years; chances are, the species that roams corporate waters will prove just as hardy.
Eric Gelman

***

The reason worry kills more people than work is that more people worry than work.
Robert Frost

***

All work and no play makes Jack a dull boy — and Jill a wealthy widow.
Evan Esar

***

In my business hours I avoid fatigue. I do this by not doing too much work — the only trustworthy recipe.
Edmund Valpy Knox

***

Work: A dangerous disorder affecting high public functionaries who want to go fishing.
Ambrose Bierce

***

"Hello."
"Is this Johnson?"
"Yes, this is Johnson."
"It doesn't sound like Johnson."
"Well it is Johnson."
"Are you sure this is Johnson?"
"Yes I am Johnson."
"Well, Johnson, this is Peterson, and we need you to write a report for us."
"I'll tell Johnson when he gets in."

***

Molly:	"That Smith is a financial genius."
Polly:	"Why?"
Molly:	"She earns money faster than her family can spend it."

***

Interviewer:	"How fast do you type?"
Applicant:	"It depends."
Interviewer:	"On what?"
Applicant:	"Whether or not the wind is with me."

***

Interviewer:	"You get five sick days a year for the first five years and then after that you get ten sick days a year."
Applicant:	"I guess the longer you work here, the sicker you get."

***

Applicant: "Do you have a retirement plan?"

Interviewer: "I'm not sure. No one has ever stayed here long
                  enough for me to find out."

***

A woman was called into the personnel office.
"I'm sorry Madge," the personnel administrator said, "but we
are firing you."
Madge became furious. "How can you fire me? You
administrators think you are really hot stuff. You spend all day behind
your desk, pushing papers, never getting anything done. You don't do
anything all day long."
The administrator waited until Madge was done and then calmly
said. "That's why we are firing you. Everyone thinks you are part of
management."

***

Applicant: "Do you manage with your heart or your head?"

Boss: "It doesn't matter. They're both made of stone."

***

Manager: "I'm the kind of guy you can't help but like."

Applicant: "Really, why is that?"

Manager: "Because if you don't I'll fire you."

***

Manager:	"Your resumé is so good we have decided to hire you without any further interviewing."
Applicant:	"Well I can't take the job."
Manager:	"Why not?"
Applicant:	"I don't want to work for any company so stupid it believes what my resumé says."

***

Bob Thompson was an hour late for a meeting. When he came into the conference room his leg was in a cast.
"Thompson, you're late," the company president yelled.
"Sorry, Sir, I slipped and fell and a car ran over my leg."
"And that took an hour?"

***

One day an employee came bursting into the personnel manager's office, his face as red as a tomato. "What's wrong, Tompkins?" the manager asked. "My manager just told me to go to hell," Tompkins replied, his face about to explode. The personnel manager walked over and put his arm around Tompkins' shoulder. "Well she had no business saying that to you. She knows you don't have any vacation time left."

***

I used to stand up for what was right -- but someone kept stealing my chair.

My career crisis is going nicely -- thank you for asking.

My job Description:

Show up every day until I retire.

My job only depresses me when I think about it.

WORKING LATE AT NIGHT
(To the tune of "Strangers in the Night")

Is there anything as lovely as someone basking in the glow of a
computer monitor at midnight?

Working late at night,
Bad circumstances,
Wondering in the night,
What were the chances,
I'll be getting home,
Before the night was through.

Something must get done,
There's no denying,
Something must get done,
There's no use crying,
Something must get done,
By me and by you.

Working in the night,
We're tired people who are,
Working in the night,
Up till the moment when the last task is all through,
No one really knew,
Just how long we'd have to stay,
And sleep would be so far away.

All through this long night,
We've been so busy,
Workers till dawn's light,
We're feeling dizzy,
We look and smell a fright,
We workers in the night.

***

One day at a business lunch an important executive was telling a very long story about his latest acquisition to a junior executive. It went on and on for almost forty minutes. Finally, the executive said, "Well, to make a long story short ——,"

"Too late," interrupted the junior executive (who has since found a new job).

* * *

One of the greatest failings of today's executive is his inability to do what he's supposed to do.
　　　Malcolm Kent

* * *

One morning Mr. Smith, the president of a Fortune 500 company, received the sad news of the sudden and unexpected death of his close friend, Mr. Thompson, who also happened to be a vice president of the same company. A few hours later, while Mr. Smith was still stunned by the news, Mr. Johnson, an aggressive, up-and-coming executive called.

"I was so sorry to hear about the death of Thompson."

"Thank you," Mr. Smith replied. "It certainly came as quite a shock."

"I wanted to let you know that I want to take Thompson's place," Mr. Johnson said boldly.

Mr. Smith, flabbergasted by the statement, replied, "Well it's okay with me if it's okay with the mortician."

* * *

Manager 1:　　　"I hate playing cards with the boss."

Manager 2:　　　"Why, does he cheat?"

Manager 1:　　　"No, but somehow you have a feeling he thinks there are five kings at the table: the heart, the spade, the club, the diamond, and him."

* * *

The world is full of willing people — some willing to work, the rest willing to let them.

    Robert Frost

* * *

In a hierarchy, every employee tends to rise to his level of incompetence.

    Laurence J. Peter

* * *

Only mediocrities rise to the top in a system that won't tolerate wavemaking.

    Laurence J. Peter

* * *

The meek may inherit the earth — but not its mineral rights.

    J. Paul Getty

* * *

In this country, when you attack the Establishment, they don't put you in jail or a mental institution. They do something worse. They make you a member of the Establishment.

    Art Buchwald

* * *

He who laughs last just realized the boss told the joke.

"Well, I for one will be happy if there's a layoff."

Helen (on the phone): "Please call maintenance right away — something's
wrong with my desk — there's no work piled on it."

* * *

John: "You can always tell who the new employees are."

Lisa: "How?"

John: "They get to work on time and take notes at
                meetings."

* * *

Jones: "Are you perplexed?"

Engdahl: "No, I'm a manager — I'm just confused."

* * *

Boss: "Are you working hard on your report?"

Kevin: "Well let me put it this way, I'm on the verge of
                mental exertion."

* * *

**Behind every successful
Supervisor there's a lot of
overworked people who
will never get any of the
credit.**

Leadership appears to be the art of getting others to want to do something you are convinced should be done.
Vance Packard

***

If all else fails, immortality can always be assured by spectacular error.
John Kenneth Galbraith

***

My father taught me to work, but not to love it. I never did like to work, and I don't deny it. I'd rather read, tell stories, crack jokes, talk, laugh — anything but work.
Abraham Lincoln

***

Nothing is really work unless you would rather be doing something else.
James M. Barrie

***

If you don't want to work you have to work to earn enough money so that you won't have to work.
Ogden Nash

***

Work consists of whatever a body is obliged to do, and play consists of whatever a body is not obliged to do.
Mark Twain

***

We should all do what, in the long run, gives us joy, even if it is only picking grapes or soiling the laundry.
E.B. White

***

Work: A necessity for man. Man invented the alarm clock.
   Pablo Picasso

     ***

Coffee is a pretty powerful stimulant. I had a friend who drank twenty cups a day at work. He died last month, but a week later he was still mingling in the company lounge.
     Milton Berle

     ***

One of the symptoms of approaching nervous breakdown is the belief that one's work is terribly important. If I were a medical man, I should prescribe a holiday to any patient who considered his work important.
     Bertrand Russell

     ***

Rick: "I mean, what AM I supposed to call you? My 'Girl Friend'? My 'Companion'? My 'Roommate'? Nothing sounds quite right!"
Joanie: "How about your 'Reason for Living'?"
Rick: "No, no. I need something I can use around the office."
     Garry Trudeau (Doonesbury)

     ***

It is easier to make a businessman out of a musician than a musician out of a businessman.
     Goddard Lieberson

     ***

There is no problem so big that management cannot create a seminar around it -- that includes lunch.

" ROUGH DAY AT THE OFFICE, DEAR ? "

Window office:	A touch of glass.
Executive lounge:	Where company bigwigs can shed their skins for a while.
Office space:	What executives stare off into.
Executive perks:	Giving someone the benefits of the clout.
Executive:	Someone who can make quick decisions, anticipate the future, coordinate multiple projects and has a helluva putt.
Executive washroom:	A 5-ply throne.
Power:	An acceptable substitute for interpersonal and social skills.
Paper clips:	Legos® for executives.
President:	Rule model.
Executive:	Someone who talks to visitors while the employees get the work done.
Divest:	What de-executive wears with de-fancy suit.
Executive suite:	A big office with an attitude.
Decision theory:	"Eeny, meany, miney, mo."
Strategy:	A corporate brass tactic.
Company car:	Corporate imposed steerility.

* * *

Johnson:	"I'm a self-made man."
Robertson:	"Well you certainly would never get past our quality control department."

* * *

Manager:	"I think you may be overworking your staff."
Supervisor:	"What makes you say that?"
Manager:	"They are wearing toe tags for name badges."

* * *

Sensible ethic:	Flushing the toilet if you have to pass gas and someone else is in the bathroom.
Lunchroom:	Where food and gossip are devoured.
Bathroom:	The corporate reading room.
Birthdays:	A socialized opportunity to goof off.
Dieter:	The person who takes the last doughnut and won't admit it.
Breakroom chatter:	Lines of assembly.
Office party:	Where fun is a four letter word.
Eccentricity:	What management cuts off if you don't help pay the bills.
Company dinner parties:	Social events with all the charm of tooth decay.
Company picnic:	Team building in a bun.
Coffee drinker:	One who's bean mugged.

Company sport teams:	Jocks of all trades.
Commute:	The slowest distance between two points.
Socializing:	Non-business related chatter that isn't being done with the person who perceives it as socializing.
Coffee break:	What no one takes so that's why they were late getting back from lunch.
Insider trading:	Switching chairs with a co-worker when they are away on vacation.

* * *

President:	"I want this report on my desk by Thursday."
Manager:	"I want a 50% raise."
President:	"What is that supposed to mean?"
Manager:	"We are both going to be disappointed."

* * *

The head of personnel called a meeting with a department manager who had rejected an applicant.

"Mr. Johnson has excellent credentials. He finished at the top of his class at Harvard, has over 10 years of experience in the field, and is a recognized authority. But you have rejected him. Why?"

"I wrote my reason down on his application," the manager replied.

"It says 'Bites nails.' Biting his nails is not a good reason not to hire him."

"Of course it is," the manager said as she stood up to leave. "He bit my nails."

* * *

Work is not
something
I would
recom-
mend to
everyone.

Why does
my boss
so often
desire
the best
when he
seldom
gets it?

Can anyone
explain why
no matter
how well I
do my job
the meat
loaf in the
cafeteria
still tastes
bad?

Bill Jones had spent years with the company. He started out in the mailroom and put himself through college at night. After years of hard work and struggling the company advanced him into a manager's position. Unfortunately, Jones forgot what it was like to be one of the "workers" and became a tyrant.

People in his department kept quitting after only a few months. Then one day Todd Bates came to work for him. Bates was a hard worker, but that wasn't enough for Jones. When Jones saw that he could order Bates around and Bates would obey his command Jones began treating Bates like a slave. Then one day Jones lost his eyesight. It seems that Jones had forgotten an old piece of wisdom — if you master Bates you'll go blind.

***

Interviewer: "Have you ever suffered from temporary insanity?"

Applicant: "No. I've usually enjoyed it."

***

Ms. Jones called one of her employees into her office for his review.

Ms. Jones: "Well, Mr. Thomas, how are you doing?"

Mr. Thomas: "Fine."

Ms. Jones: "That's what you think."

***

Applicant: "My last employer said I reminded her of a computer."

Interviewer: "Because of your ability to process information quickly?"

Applicant: "No, because neither of us could think on our own."

***

Interviewer:	"It says here you have been with the Acme Corporation for 8 years but have only 6 years of experience."
Applicant:	"Well, I was late a lot."

* * *

Jones:	"Personnel treats me like an old comforter."
Everly:	"How?"
Jones:	"Every time I ask for a raise, they turn me down."

* * *

Employee 1:	"I see we are about to have another change in office policy."
Employee 2:	"How do you know that?"
Employee 1:	"The boss's son just broke a rule."

* * *

Personnel:	"Whom should we notify in case of an emergency?"
New employee:	"A doctor."

* * *

Holiday:	Grown-up recess.
Play along:	The ability to walk on eggshells while wearing combat boots and carrying an elephant.
Office laughter:	Often prevented by practicing mirth control.

Office snoop:	An automatic teller.
Stock options:	When the office kitchen has both beef and chicken broth.
Vacation:	Something that is more work to go on and get back from than it was worth.
Golf:	An excuse to have the flu.
Gone fishing:	A slaving withdrawal.
Morale:	Something that is affected by office atmospheric pressure.
Organic structure:	That stuff growing in the coffee cup no one will return to the kitchen.
Office collections:	The one time every employee is asked to contribute.
Whiner:	Someone with a bad case of the snivels.
Motivators:	Cheerleaders in sweater vests.
Office politics:	Top dancing.
Motivational seminars:	Places where people are away from work to learn how to be more productive at work.

If you aren't feeling guilty you are an overachiever.

"WE'RE REPLACING YOU, DALTON, BUT I'D LIKE TO HAVE YOU
STAY ON FIFTEEN MINUTES TO TELL THE NEW MAN WHAT
YOU KNOW ABOUT YOUR JOB."

Microwave:	The only place where things heat up faster than in the board room.
Office gossiper:	Someone with bad circulation.
Office diplomacy:	Non-offensive lying.
Water cooler:	H2Oh did you hear about...
Clock:	The only thing in the office we want to get ticked off.
Bowling team:	Where employers encourage employees to strike.
Conformity:	Waving the pinstriped flag of surrender.
Cliques:	Unofficial gossip committees.
Doughnuts:	Large morning pills.
Car pool:	A group of people driven to madness and then back home at the end of the day.
Ass-covering:	Strategic gymnastics.
Liability:	How comfortable an office couch is for taking a nap.

People who work in glass offices can never scratch where it itches.

PerformanceAnalysis:	Office gossip.
Expectancy theory:	Pregnancy rumors.
Bulletin board:	Office hang-ups.
Ass kissing:	Strategic aerobics.
Grapevine:	Disassembly line.

***

Geri:	"I heard through the grapevine you are getting a big promotion."
Terri:	"Yeah, I started the rumor."
Geri:	"Why?"
Terri:	"Well they aren't too bright in management and I'm hoping when they hear it they will think they started it."

***

Sales Rep 1:	"I think I may be spending too much time traveling."
Sales Rep 2:	"What makes you say that?"
Sales Rep 1:	"The Hare Krishnas at 15 major airports know me by name."

***

LOOKING FOR A NEW JOB

1.   A letter of application will get stuck in with other correspondence you give your boss to sign.

2.   As soon as you get a call about an interview your boss will come and stand by your desk.

3.   If you have an interview over lunch, you will surely get a rush project.

4.   If you answer a blind ad to a P.O. box it will be your company.

5.   The person you interview with will be related to your boss.

6.   You will get a call back on the job you really want the day after you accept a different job.

7.   Your supervisor will sneak up on you while you have your resumé on your computer screen.

8.   The person you give as a reference will have had an affair with the spouse of the person who interviews you.

9.   Just as the director of personnel comes into the lobby the receptionist will ask if she knows you from treatment.

10.   The clammier your hand, the drier the hand of the person you shake hands with.

***

There is never anyone near a door when you have your hands full of files.

WORK is a four letter word.

What is this "Career" I keep READING about?

I wish my boss was more like me... I'm so understanding when I do something wrong.

YOU KNOW YOUR JOB IS IN JEOPARDY WHEN...

1.   You see it advertised in the paper — and you haven't quit.

2.   Your boss gives you a gift certificate for a resumé service.

3.   Your supervisor puts an empty carton by your desk and suggests you hang on to it... just in case.

4.   Your nameplate disappears and they tell you they can't afford to replace it.

5.   You ask for more business cards and they give you a dozen.

6.   Other people in the office start asking you if your chair is comfortable.

7.   Your IN box is empty and no one cares.

8.   You haven't been asked to serve on a committee for at least a week.

9.   You are told the wrong place to go for the company picnic.

10.   Buzzards are circling your parking spot.

***

The following memo was sent to department managers:

"Here is your yearly budget. We aren't going to be able to give you the money we allotted you but we expect you to keep track of where it goes."

***

(WORKING IN A) BOSSLESS WONDERLAND
(To the tune of "Winter Wonderland")

When the cad's away the peons will play!!!!!!!

Phone bells ring,
Can you hear 'em?
We'd pick them up,
But we're not near 'em.
It's a wonderful day,
The boss is away,
Working in a Bossless Wonderland.

There's work,
But why do it,
Soon enough,
We'll get to it.
The place is alive,
You'd think it was five,
Working in a Bossless Wonderland.

In the breakroom we will hold a party,
And laugh about the people we work for,
We'll cut loose and act so darn foolhardy,
'Cause who knows when we'll have this chance once more.

Later on we may get fired,
For what has transpired.
But we'll still have some fun,
'Till this day is done,
Working in a Bossless Wonderland.

***

Secretary:	"I think my new boss may be a little immature for such a tough job."
Personnel:	"Why do you say that?"
Secretary:	"He canceled his subscription to The Kiplinger Report because it didn't have a funnies section."

* * *

Secretary:	"Everyone in the company is mad at you."
Office Manager:	"When I took this job I knew I would make unpopular decisions."
Secretary:	"Well people agree that this is the second most unpopular decision you've made."
Office Manager:	"What was the first?"
Secretary:	"Taking the job in the first place."

* * *

The Acme Corporation hired a former kindergarten teacher as its new personnel director. At first it was hard for her to make the transition. At her first staff meeting she told the employees that when she held up one finger it meant be quiet, two fingers meant take your seats, and three fingers meant free time. She changed her approach when all week long she saw one employee after another telling her to be quiet — but with the wrong finger. So she fixed them. They had to sit in the corner of the conference room and take a 15 minute-timeout instead of a coffee break.

* * *

YOU KNOW YOU WORK IN A DUMP WHEN:

1.   There is a Sears catalog in every bathroom stall.

2.   Your business cards have ads on the back.

3.   Your office is smaller than the handicapped stall in the bathroom.

4.   You are given a paper clip allotment.

5.   The company cafeteria is featured in a Health Department training film.

6.   OSHA has a regional office in your building.

7.   Mike Wallace has his own parking space.

8.   The Christmas party invitation asks if you want a hamburger, cheeseburger or chicken McNuggets for dinner.

9.   The company president's mother is the receptionist.

10.   Your secretary is a regular guest of Geraldo.

***

I was just starting to win the rat race and then they went and bought a new cat.

CEO: "Whenever I think of how all my employees are struggling to get by on their paychecks it really upsets me. So, I have made an important decision."

Vice President: "You are going to give everyone a raise?"

CEO: "No. I'm going to stop thinking about it."

* * *

Jr. Executive: "I am a very determined person."

Sr. Executive: "Really, give me an example."

Jr. Executive: "Whenever I'm faced with a difficult job I determine who I can order to do it for me, and then I give it to them."

* * *

Jr. Executive: "What is the key to success as an executive?"

Sr. Executive: "Having the ability to get the credit for all the hard work everyone else does."

* * *

On the day you finally finish all your filing, you will be given a new assignment.

CEO:	"How many branches do we have?"
Executive Asst:	"Six."
CEO:	"Enumerate them."
Executive Asst:	"One, two, three, four, five, six."

* * *

Executive 1:	"I had a great day — I made a lot of connections."
Executive 2:	"Yeah, I didn't do anything all day either."

* * *

YOU KNOW IT'S A CLASSY PLACE TO WORK WHEN:

1. There are violinists strolling through the cafeteria.

2. The toilet paper is triple ply.

3. You need a reservation to get a table in the break room.

4. The president's wife screens potential mistresses.

5. They sell gray pinstripe Depends® in the company store.

6. The Christmas party is held in Bethlehem.

7. Your computer has a secretary.

8. You can choose the currency in which you want your paycheck issued.

9. Your company badge is also an American Express® Gold Card.

10. There's a helicopter pad on the roof — of the president's car.

* * *

Jr. Executive:	"Take it easy. If you're not careful you will have a heart attack."
Sr. Executive:	"I don't have heart attacks — I give heart attacks."

* * *

Jr. Executive:	"So what does a vice president in this company do?"
Vice President:	"Read a lot of memos and keep a close eye on the company president's health."

* * *

Boss:	"This is a very difficult assignment. How do you plan on approaching the problem?"
Jr. Executive:	"Head on. I'm going to take it and 'head on' down to someone else's office and give it to them."

* * *

Controller:	"Well the books don't look good — we're going to have to tighten our belt."
President:	"Tighten our belt!?! Again?!? I already have an ingrown buckle."

* * *

Jones:	"I feel like a turkey in November."
Smith:	"Why?"
Jones:	"I have my review today."

* * *

Interviewer:	"So tell me a little about yourself."
Applicant:	"Well at my last job I made a suggestion that saved the company $40,000 a year."
Interviewer:	"How wonderful. How did they save all that money?"
Applicant:	"After reading my suggestion they fired me."

* * *

Personnel:	"I think I found the perfect manager for the sales department."
President:	"What makes you say that?"
Personnel:	"He used to train pit bulls."

* * *

Interviewer:	"We give all employees a beeper so they can come any time we call."
Applicant:	"Do you also give them a flea collar and rubber bone to chew on?"

* * *

Interviewer:	"He is looking for a secretary who comes in early, works late, never makes mistakes, takes initiative, doesn't complain and can work under extreme pressure without letting it get to her."
Applicant:	"I think your only hope of filling this job is to enroll Mother Teresa in typing school."

* * *

"WHAT A DAY! THE COMPUTER BROKE DOWN
AND WE ALL HAD TO THINK!"

Our company has a new employee benefit plan — it's called "Neglect."

***

A personnel manager called one of the bookkeepers into her office. "Jim, you are a very good worker and we would hate to lose you, but you are always late. If you don't start getting here on time we will have to let you go."

"I know I am late," Jim explained, "I have a difficult time getting going in the morning."

"Well, don't forget," the personnel manager went on, "the early bird catches the worm."

"No offense," Jim replied, "but a worm isn't much motivation to get out of bed."

***

Working with people is difficult, but not impossible.
    Peter Drucker

***

Job Seeker: A want addict.
    Leonard Levinson

***

If you pay peanuts, you get monkeys.
    James Goldsmith

***

Punctuality is the virtue of the bored.
    Evelyn Waugh

***

I've always been worried about people who are willing to work for nothing. Sometimes that's all you get from them, nothing.
    Sam Ervin

***

You Know Your Review Isn't Going Well When....

1.   You hear "Taps" being played as you enter the room.

2.   You are offered a cigarette and a blindfold.

3.   A security officer is standing in the corner.

4.   You are given an agenda and it includes a lunch break.

5.   Your boss brings an overhead projector into the room.

6.   Your performance review sheet is marked "Exhibit 1."

7.   There is a box of industrial strength Kleenex® on the table.

8.   The first question is "Did you take your Prozac® today?"

9.   You are asked to come into the conference room — and to bring your coat.

10.   Your supervisor asks to look at your bus schedule.

* * *

A lot of fellows nowadays have a B.A., M.D., or Ph.D. Unfortunately, they don't have a J.O.B.
    Fats Domino

* * *

Greg: "Have you heard the latest joke about the CEO?"

Peg: "I am the CEO!"

Greg: "That's okay, I'll tell it slowly and use small words."

* * *

Male Exec: "Do you want to be my equal someday?"

Female Jr. Exec: "No — I have ambition."

* * *

A rather large CEO came into his bookkeeping office and demanded to know where all the profits had gone. The accountant suggested he stand sideways in front of the mirror."

* * *

Boss: Spelled backwards a double SOB.
>Leonard Levinson

* * *

Businessman's Lunch: Something to hold down a couple of martinis.
>Leonard Levinson

* * *

Nothing is so embarrassing as watching your boss do something you assured him couldn't be done.
>Earl Wilson

* * *

The mark of a true executive is usually illegible.
>Leo J. Farrell, Jr.

* * *

He's fair. He treats us all the same — like dogs.
>Henry Jordan

* * *

By working faithfully eight hours a day, you may eventually get to be a boss and work twelve hours a day.
Robert Frost

***

The trouble with the rat race is even if you win, you're still a rat.
Lily Tomlin

***

Supervisor:	A dictator but without a sense of humor.
Position:	Stations of the boss.
Work:	Something to do when you can't get to sleep.
Action:	A force of nature precipitated by the impending presence of an authority figure.
Apprentice:	A relative of the boss.
Span of control:	Refers to how far away an employee is from the visual and/or audio detection of the boss.
Late:	Arriving at work after your boss does.

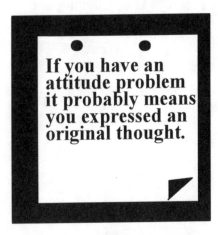

If you have an attitude problem it probably means you expressed an original thought.

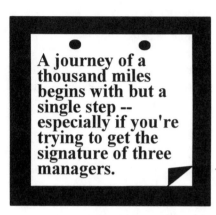

A journey of a thousand miles begins with but a single step -- especially if you're trying to get the signature of three managers.

Good management: Keeping the employees who hate you away from the employees who are still undecided.

Decentralization: Employees scattering when the boss comes in the room.

Mental health day: A vocation vacation.

Job motivation: A desk right outside the boss's office.

Behavior modification: The boss is in the room.

Brown noser: Someone too cowardly to fight and too incompetent to find another job.

Bosstard: A bastard you work for.

Boss: Called an overseer until the Emancipation Proclamation was issued.

***

MY BOSS THINKS HE'S CASANOVA
(To the tune of "Blame It on the Bossanova")

If Stephen King wants to write a really scary novel he should write "Mid-Life" about a man who reaches 50 and decides to "start living!"

I was at my desk,
When he spilled the news,
He had left his wife,
He had the mid-life blues,
He began to change,
He really was gung-ho,
And pretty soon he was acting quite macho.

My boss thinks he's Casanova,
With his bright red car,
My boss thinks he's Casanova,
At the single bars.
Well it all began when he hit the big five-oh,
Now he's learning how to disco,
My boss thinks he's Casanova,
The dream of fools.

Now he drinks herb tea,
Just like a Casanova,
And he's working out,
Just like a Casanova,
And he's eating brie,
Just like a Casanova.
And alfalfa sprouts.

***

This job is like a bean bag chair -- hard to get into it and impossible to get out of with any dignity at all.

Manager:	"I deserve a raise."
Vice President:	"Why?"
Manager:	"I'm doing the work of three people."
Vice President:	"Give me the other two individuals' names and I'll fire 'em."

* * *

Every year the CEO complained that his desk was too small, and every year it was replaced with a larger and more expensive one. Finally, one year after the CEO had issued his annual desk complaint the office manager came to discuss it with him.

"Sir," the manager said, "perhaps it would be easier if you told me what size desk you think you would be happy with and then we wouldn't have to order a new one each year."

"Well," the CEO replied, "order me the first desk you find that is mahogany, hand-carved, has plenty of drawer space, and comes with its own zip code."

* * *

Executive:	"It's time for me to go to a convention."
Secretary:	"Do you need to learn about a new product or technology?"
Executive:	"No, I need to unload some of my business cards."

* * *

President:	"I ordered piped-in music to improve office morale."
Personnel:	"Well, sir, I don't think that will improve morale."
President:	"Sure it will. After a couple of months I'll have it turned off and that will make everyone happier."

* * *

This job
is like a
big
party
and I'm
the
pinata.

There
must be
more to
work
than this
or why
do i keep
showing
up?

**There is a
difference
of opinion
about
whether on
not our
company is
working as
a team.**

CEO:	"I'm going to form a committee to find a solution to our financial problem."
Assistant:	"Gee, why don't you do something easy first, like get the Pope to go out on a date with you?"

* * *

President:	"Wilson, it has come to my attention that you are impossible to get along with and that everyone in the company hates you."
Wilson:	"Yes sir, I'm afraid that is true."
President:	"How do you justify your actions?"
Wilson:	"Someday I want your job."

* * *

After a long illness the owner of a company died. He was a hard man to work for and always complaining about one thing or another. At his funeral the employees of the company were talking about how unhappy he had always been and how critical he was of everything.

"Well, maybe he has finally found some peace in Heaven," said one of the vice presidents.

His secretary, who had taken the greatest brunt of his miserable attitude shook her head. "I doubt it," she said, "He probably has found fault with God."

* * *

It's the little things that count -- but enough about my salary.

Tyler:	"He's a self-made man."
Reed:	"Really?"
Tyler:	"Yes, and he worships his maker!"

* * *

Wife 1:	"I can always tell when it's budget time at the office."
Wife 2:	"How?"
Wife 1:	"My husband wants 3.5-play before sex."

* * *

The owner of a company decided to use the popular phrase "Just Do It" as a motto to increase productivity in his company. He went to a graphic design consultant to have her create posters with the words on it that would not only catch the workers' eyes but would inspire them to greater things.

After the posters were designed and printed the owner had them placed all over the building. A few weeks later the graphic designer stopped by to see the owner and check up on the results of the productivity campaign. When she arrived she found not even one sign posted.

"What happened?" she inquired. "Didn't the employees become more productive?"

"Well the posters worked too well," the owner said, a number of veins popping out of his neck.

"How could they work too well?" the designer asked.

"I had them up for a week. By the end of the week my secretary had quit to become a professional golfer, my accountant stole all my money, two of my stock boys went to L.A. to become comedy writers, and every day someone wrote 'Eat Me' on my car."

* * *

President: "If we don't get rid of this piped-in music I will never get any work done."

Office Manager: "But sir, if the music bothers you just shut your door and you won't hear it at all."

President: "That's not the problem."

Office Manager: "Well then, what is the problem?"

President: "Every time they play some song by Barry Manilow my secretary starts crying and I can't get a thing done."

***

Boss: "Johnson, why are you sitting at your desk reading the newspaper?"

Johnson: "I didn't hear you coming."

***

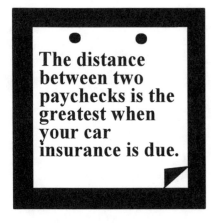

The distance between two paychecks is the greatest when your car insurance is due.

"It's quite simple—you just have to know where to look."

Miller:	"My secretary has a terrible memory."
Freeman:	"She forgets everything?"
Miler:	"No, she never forgets anything."

***

Secretary:	"You've been in your office all day. What have you been doing?"
Boss:	"Preparing an impromptu speech for tonight's company banquet."

***

Secretary to her aging boss:	"Why don't you get a hearing aid?"
Boss:	"I don't need it; I hear more now than I want to."

***

Boss:	"Why didn't you come into my office when I buzzed you?"
Secretary:	"I didn't hear you buzz."
Boss:	"Well, the next time you don't hear me buzz, please come into my office."

* * *

Boss:	"You are always complaining that you don't have any money. If you saved ten dollars a week how long would it be before you had a hundred dollars?"
Secretary:	"Never. There's a sweater I want that costs $85."

* * *

Boss 1:	"Does it bother you if your secretary tells fibs?"
Boss 2:	"No — it bothers me if she tells the truth."

* * *

Secretary:	"My boss gets along with everyone."
Boss:	"She must be really nice."
Secretary:	"No, she's a coward."

* * *

Secretary:	"My boss's office is such a pig pen that when I come out the company makes me wipe my feet so I don't track dirt into the rest of the office."

* * *

> **CEOs are like bills -- they arrive every day and no one is happy to see them.**

Boss: "What did you think of my speech at the company banquet?"

Secretary: "It made me want to clap my hands — over my ears."

***

Boss: "Can you take shorthand?"

Secretary: "Yes, but it takes me longer."

***

Manager 1: "Is your new secretary really slow?"

Manager 2: "Yes. It takes her two hours to watch '60 Minutes.'"

***

Tracy: "My boss is a real bitch — no one can stand her."

Sandy: "Oh, she can't be that bad."

Tracy: "Well, once she was in a beauty contest and Miss Congeniality slapped her."

***

I use to do my best but it kept arousing suspicion.

If only my work was as good as my resume.

If we could look up men's pants there'd be no glass ceiling.

Terry:	"What was all that yelling?"
Larry:	"My boss is suffering in silence again."

***

Mr. Jones:	"How do you think I keep my youth?"
Ms. Wells:	"You buy her gifts and promise to leave your wife."

***

Boss:	"Well, I've changed my mind."
Secretary:	"I hope this one works better than the last one."

***

Boss:	"Don't you know the difference between accept and except?"
Secretary:	"Sure."
Boss:	"But you always type the wrong one."
Secretary:	"Well, at least I'm consistent."

***

Boss:	"You didn't spell this word correctly."
Secretary:	"Sorry. I spell by ear and I have a hearing impairment."

***

The more office supplies you have in your bag, the more likely it will break and spill its contents in the company parking lot.

Victor:	"Why is the office building so tall?"
Victoria:	"So the company president can be as close to God as he already thinks he is."

* * *

Boss (on deathbed):	"I know I was a cruel and unpopular employer. I suppose no one will even show up for my funeral."
Sr. VP:	"Oh don't worry, Sir, I'm sure everyone in the company will be there. After all, if you give the people what they want they are sure to show up."

* * *

VP:	"How do you get your employees to work on time?"
President:	"Well, I have 30 employees, and every morning I bring in two dozen doughnuts."

* * *

Ms. Thompson:	"My company is looking for an accountant."
Mr. Harris:	"Didn't you just hire one?"
Ms.Thompson:	"Yep, and that's the one we're looking for."

***

Boss:	All right all you idiots, back to work."
	(Everyone but Tom returns to their desks.)
Boss:	"Well.......?"
Tom:	"There sure are a lot of idiots working here, aren't there?"

***

Boss:	"You misspelled MISSISSIPPI."
Secretary:	"Oh, you must have meant the state, not the river."

***

Never buy stock in the company you work for. It will cause you to worry about the lousy work you're turning out.

I could do great things in my job if I weren't so busy covering my butt.

I know what it is like to be happy in your job -- I've seen pictures of it.

I just finished six months of research and now I can't find where I put the damn question.

Boss:	"Well I must say, Mr. Jones, you never make the same mistake twice."
Mr. Jones:	"Thank you, Ma'am."
Boss:	"No, you are forever finding new ways to make mistakes."

***

Boss 1:	"I hate my computer."
Boss 2:	"Why?"
Boss 1:	"It isn't living in constant fear of being fired."

***

Wendy:	"My secretary has come up with a new filing system — if a letter is to Mr. Jones of the Fortune Company she files it under M."
Wendell:	"For Mister?"
Wendy:	"No, for mail."

***

Ms. Johnson:	"I had to fire my secretary. She was always on the phone with her boyfriend."
Mr. Thomas:	"Did it affect her work?"
Ms. Johnson:	"No, it was my husband."

***

If your boss says you have promise... you better start packing up your things.

Secretary:	"Sir, the Riverside Nursing Home just called about your donation."
Boss:	"What did they want?"
Secretary:	"When they asked for donations they didn't mean your parents. You're supposed to go and pick them up."

* * *

Allen:	"We're taking up a collection for a going-away gift for the boss."
Beth:	"I didn't know he was planning on leaving."
Allen:	"He isn't, but we figured it was worth a try!"

* * *

Expense accounts:	Often a bunk statement.
Foreman:	Supervisor with a hard hat.
Administration:	A place where creativity goes to die.
Handshake:	Pectoral pumping.
Forecasting:	A gypsy with an MBA.

Fast track:	A junior executive with a set of goals to meet and a stack of bills to pay.
Express management:	People with six ideas or less.
Faking it:	Something equally effective in the bedroom and boardroom.
Corporate ladder:	Something that has rarely rung true.
Computer programmers:	DOSigners.
Attitude:	A staff infection.
Balance the books:	Creative writing.
Beeper:	An electronic device that when activated in a crowd alerts one person and annoys everyone else.

***

Workers: The person who goes to work before 9 a.m.
     Anonymous

Workers: Those who look at the clock the most often.
     Anonymous

***

The bigger a hurry you are in, the more paper clips will be stuck together.

Files are the curse of modern civilization. I had a young secretary once. Just out of school. I told her "If you can keep these files straight, I'll marry you." She did, and so I married her.
    Fiorello LaGuardia

* * *

Job: Death without dignity.
    Dylan Thomas

* * *

Work is the hardest way to make a living.
    Anonymous (and every secretary on the face of the Earth)

* * *

All the secretaries hunch at their IBMs, snickering at keys. What they know could bring down the government.
    Robin Morgan ("On the Watergate Women")

* * *

There's only one way to work — like hell.
    Bette Davis

* * *

The most important thing I have ever learned about management is that the work must be done by other men.
    Alfred P. Sloan, Jr.

..... and then redone by secretaries so it is correct.
    Mary Hirsch

* * *

Yesterday I was a dog. Today I'm a dog. Tomorrow I'll probably still be a dog. Sigh. There's so little hope for advancement.
Snoopy

* * *

Zelda: "There's always a surge of energy here around 9:30."

Susan: "Because everyone has had their coffee?"

Zelda: "No, that's when the boss arrives."

* * *

Ms. Perkins watched while her secretary was on the phone for ten minutes without saying anything. Finally she hung up. "Who were you on the phone with?" she asked.
"It was an obscene phone call," the secretary replied.
"Well, why didn't you hang up right away?"
"I needed a breather."

* * *

Bosses aren't off the rack, they're made to order — and order — and order....

* * *

"Okay. That's my proposed benefit package," said the Boss. "But, I am not an ogre. I want all of you to vote on it. All opposed raise their hands and say 'I Quit.'"

* * *

Secretary 1:   "My boss got where he is the tough way."

Secretary 2:   "Hard work?"

Secretary 1:   "No, being nice to his dad."

* * *

"It's a photograph of the little woman . . .
serves as a constant incentive."

Boss:	"Please don't tell anybody what I'm paying you."
Secretary:	"Oh, I won't, I'm ashamed of my salary, too"

* * *

Jack:	"My boss is pigheaded."
Jill:	"Why?"
Jack:	"He thinks there is only one way to spell a word."

* * *

Secretary:	"I have to go home. I'm schizophrenic."
Boss:	"That makes four of us."

* * *

Boss:	"I'm looking for the perfect computer."
Salesman:	"What does it have to do?"
Boss:	"Kiss up and laugh at my jokes."

* * *

Intrapreneur:	Entrepreneur spelled wrong.
Chairman:	A male with delusions of being a chair with super powers.
CEO:	Certified.
Chair:	An ass-sit in any company.
Born executive:	Someone whose parent owns the company.

Hierarchy:	A WASP totem-pole.
Innovation:	What the board of directors wants — as long as everyone else is doing it.
Credenza:	A walnut toy chest for executives.
Vice presidents:	The next best thing to being heir.
Board:	A long piece of wood (with a bunch of people who think they are important sitting around it).
Comptroller:	The big wheel of fortune.
Decision tree:	Where the sap rises.

***

Secretary:	"I quit."
Boss:	"Why?"
Secretary:	"I can't work for such a neat freak."
Boss:	"I'm not that big a neat freak."
Secretary:	"Then why do you make me put your messages in zip-lock bags?"

***

Boss:	"Shirley, come in here immediately."
Shirley:	"Just a minute sir, nature is calling."
Boss:	"Take a message. I need you right now."

***

A group of workers had been putting in 16-hour days and working six days a week to meet an impossible deadline. As the day when the project was due grew closer, one of the employees was so exasperated by the impossibility of the tasks still needing to be completed that when the boss arrived at work he announced:

"Sir, we are working as hard as we can, but there is no way we can finish this project by the deadline you have set."

The boss, not a person to take such a response well, bellowed, "We will miss this deadline over my dead body."

"Please," the worker replied, "don't try to cheer us up."

***

Supervisor: "My secretary's filing system is SHIT!"

Jones: "What a horrible thing to say!"

Supervisor: "Why? Her system is: Somewhere Here I Think."

***

Secretary: "So what did you get out of the convention?"

Boss: "Nothing that can't be cured with penicillin."

***

Today is the tomorrow you worried about yesterday -- and you will be docked for.

"J.B. REALLY KNOWS HOW TO MIX BUSINESS WITH PLEASURE!"

If you want to meet an honest person, go to an office supply store and see who actually buys paper clips to use at home.

Boss: "Everyone seemed to be having such a good time at the company picnic. There were smiles and laughter everywhere. I wonder how we could keep that attitude going here at the office."

Secretary: "Well, you could wear plaid shorts and black socks everyday."

* * *

Flextime: Being sure someone is there when the boss isn't playing golf.

Filing cabinet: A tall wastebasket, with drawers.

Filing: A bitcher's mound.

Doing personal work: The reason God created split screen computers.

In-box: Heap labor.

Typing: Strokes of genius.

Spelling verifier: That anal retentive secretary that loves to point out everyone's mistakes.

Bottom line: What enlarges as secretary's spread sets in.

To err is human; to overlook it is against corporate policy.

Steno pad:	Where hep secretaries crash after splitting the salt mines, daddy-o.
Shorthand:	Write on and on and on and on and on….
Secretary's day:	A ritualistic practice designed to replace raises with roses.
Memory:	What you want in a computer and don't want in a secretary.
Crisis:	What makes Friday afternoons so exciting.
Rush:	A project that never needs to be done unless it is close to the end of the day.
Steno pool:	Drown town.
Secretary:	Someone who takes your word for it.
Stenographers:	Secretaries who can type two projects at one time (a prerequisite for 99.9% of all jobs).
Buzzer:	The line that roars.
Keyboard:	A typewriter before men had to use it.

Candy dish:	The closest to a suite most secretaries will get.
Transcriber:	Going through a phrase.
Temp:	Hire today; gone tomorrow.
Administrative assistant:	A secretary with a good wardrobe.
Expandable folder:	The one time you can tell your boss to stuff it and not get in trouble.
Balance sheet:	When you have two bosses and have to take sheet from both of them.
White out:	Error freshener.
Poor typist:	Someone who is all errors.
Poor filing:	A lost art.
Personal calls:	What you never have time to make at home.

* * *

Boss:	"How was your vacation?"
Manager:	"It was great to get away from it all."
Boss:	"Well, we're glad to have you back and, by the way, 'it all' has been waiting for you in your office."

* * *

One day at a time -- and a lot of folders labeled "Hold."

I ENJOY BEING YOUR GIRL
(To the tune of "I Enjoy Being a Girl")

Isn't it nice to know that no matter how old we are, at the office we will always be "girls"? Here's a sarcastic little ditty just right for the girls" to sing around the microwave.

When you have a big job that's due,
And the office is in a whirl,
I just crank it up to warp two,
I enjoy being your girl.

When I ask you for more money,
And you laugh like I'm Milton Berle,
I just take it like a honey,
I enjoy being your girl.

I flip when you flex your corporate power,
I swoon keeping up your hectic pace,
I take messages by the hour,
And keep a happy look upon my face.

I'm strictly an office female,
And my future I hope will be,
In the employ of a free male,
Who enjoys being a boss,
Having a girl, like me!

* * *

There are no simple answers -- stupid questions yes, but no simple answers.

The buck stops here... and dies from lack of attention.

Secretary 1:	"Well, we can't stand here all day doing nothing."
Secretary 2:	"Why not?"
Secretary 1:	"People will think we are supervisors."

* * *

Boss:	"You are truly indispensable."
Secretary:	"Thank you."
Boss:	"Now all we have to do is figure out to what."

* * *

Supervisor:	"Whom are you calling?"
Secretary:	"Ralph Nader."
Supervisor:	"Why?"
Secretary:	"Mr. Jones just told me he was a self-made man and I want to have him recalled."

* * *

"WOULD YOU PLEASE MUMBLE THAT LAST SENTENCE AGAIN..."

The size of the run in your pantyhose is in direct proportion to how long before you can go buy another pair.

Boss:	"Where's Miller?"
Secretary:	"He had to be taken to the hospital."
Boss:	"Why?"
Secretary:	"He got his middle finger caught in the suggestion box."

***

Secretary 1:	"My boss has really turned himself around."
Secretary 2:	"How?"
Secretary 1:	"He used to be mean and nasty."
Secretary 2:	"And now?"
Secretary 1:	"He's nasty and mean."

***

If you have a pen
and a tampon in
your desk drawer,
you will pull out
the tampon when
your boss asks for
a pen.

The vice president was being examined by the company doctor for insurance.

"Have you ever had a serious illness?" the doctor asked.

"No."

"Have you ever had an accident?"

"No."

"You've never had an accident?"

"No. But last year I was hit by a car."

"Well, don't you think that was an accident?"

"No, my secretary did it on purpose."

***

A rather untidy secretary arrived at her desk one morning to find her boss standing there waiting.

"Look at this desk," he said, "were you raised in a barn?"

"Well, yes, I was raised on a farm." The secretary answered and then sat down and began to cry.

"I'm sorry," said the boss, "I didn't mean to hurt your feelings."

"You didn't hurt my feelings but listening to you makes me homesick for my pet donkey."

***

Boss: "I'm a confirmed bachelor. I have only myself to please."

Secretary: "Well, God knows, that's a job and a half."

***

Donna:	"My secretary types like lightning."
Barbara:	"You mean she's fast?"
Donna:	"I mean she never strikes the right letter twice."

***

Secretary:	"Boss you are a lucky man."
Boss:	"Why is that?"
Secretary:	"You won't have to buy me a new calendar, I'm still working on this year's projects."

***

Boss to secretary staring into space:	"A penny for your thoughts!"
Secretary:	"You're right; I was thinking of my salary."

***

Secretary:	"Sir, is it true money talks?"
Boss:	"It certainly is."
Secretary:	"Well my checking account could use a better conversation every two weeks or so."

***

Today is the first day of the rest of my life -- which explains my beginner's wages.

United
We
Stand...
Divided
We
Form
A Task
Force.

What I
learn
here will
last
forever
but so
will
herpes!

**Tomorrow is
another
day....
And boy do
I hope it's
better than
this one.**

Secretary 1:	"Why are we redoing this report for the 15th time?"
Secretary 2:	"Orders."
Secretary 1:	"From headquarters?"
Secretary 2:	"From hindquarters."

***

Secretary 1:	"Mr. Ross is a very sensitive man. Management doesn't like to criticize him."
Secretary 2:	"Really?"
Secretary 1:	"Yes. When he does something wrong they criticize me and he changes his ways."

***

Boss:	"I was reading that humor in the workplace can relieve stress. What could help me bring some humor into my office?"
Secretary:	"Get a mirror."

***

Secretary 1:	"When I applied for this job Mr. Jones asked if my punctuation was good."
Secretary 2:	"What did you tell him?"
Secretary 1:	"I said I'm always on time."

***

"Will you hold please? I'll see if he's in"

(Are you in?)

"I'm sorry, sir, he's out"

* * *

The receptionist is by definition underpaid to lie.
    Poems by Karen Brodine

* * *

Receptionist:	Head of the meet market.
Receptionist:	Someone who is romancing the phone.
Switchboard:	A booming buzzness.
Switchboard:	A spot with more flashing than a playground.
Switchboard operator:	A hear raiser.
Lobby:	Where a company tries to impress a client before they learn the truth.

* * *

Always carry a file and walk quickly if you want people to think you're too busy to help them.

You know your company is planning to make a major change in their health insurance coverage when they put a faith healer on staff.

HECTIC PACE
(To the tune of "Baby Face")

Do you think someday Jane Fonda will do a workout video on how to aerobically run around the office looking for this file, that letter and other assorted objects only to discover after wasting hours "on the hunt" that everything was in your boss's office all the time (probably under his copy of the "Sports Illustrated" swimsuit edition)?

Hectic pace,
I'm trying to keep up with your
Hectic pace.
It feels just like an Olympic race,
This hectic pace,
My heart is really straining,
It's like aerobic training.

Hectic pace,
I'm sweating bullets
When I'm rushing round this place.
I didn't need such stress,
I could do with much less,
Than this horrid hectic pace.

***

"LET ME GET THIS STRAIGHT. YOU SAY I COULD SAVE 62-PER CENT BY MOVING MY PLANT TO MEXICO AND BAKING 'EM THERE?"

The customer's always right, my boys,
The customer's always right.
The son-of-a-bitch
Is probably rich
So smile with all your might.
      Noel Coward

* * *

Client:	A patron saint.
Customer:	The person who is always right when they are within hearing distance.
Visitor:	The person who looks happy to be here.
Competition:	When you vie, vie again.

* * *

Boss:	"How are our accounts receivable coming?"
Bookkeeper:	"Well I don't want to alarm you, but the PAID IN FULL stamp was lost for two weeks before I noticed."

* * *

Bookkeeper:	"When we say we want our bill paid by the 10th we don't mean by the 10th notice."

* * *

Mr. Smith:	"I think Ms. Thompson may be too young to be planning our company's open house for new clients."
Ms. Jones:	"Why?"
Mr. Smith:	"I just heard her on the phone asking the liquor store what wine goes best with Twinkies and HoHos."

* * *

Pushy Customer:	"I hope I'm not too late."
Executive:	"No, don't worry, you can never get here late enough."

* * *

Client:	"How many people work in your company?"
Boss:	"About half of them."

* * *

A customer was shown into the office of the company president. It had just been remodeled and the president was trying to impress the customer with all the furnishings.

"This is a replica of a desk King Louis used. And this is a real suit of armor. And this chair is just like the one Queen Victoria used when serving tea."

The customer, duly impressed, remarked, "All you need is a moat and an alligator to keep out the enemy."

"I don't need a moat," the president replied, "I have a secretary."

* * *

Receptionist:	"Our president doesn't lie, cheat, steal or even cuss out anyone."
Client:	"That sounds like a wonderful person. How does he manage to be so good?"
Receptionist:	"He has employees who lie, cheat, steal and cuss out people for him."

* * *

Client:	"This report is incorrect."
Manager:	"You are wrong, Ms. Thomas. The report is absolutely correct."
Client:	"Remember this — the customer is always right!"
Manager:	"Yeah, that's great. It takes a lot of stress off of me."

***

Client:	"I guess the slower economy has hit your business rather hard."
President:	"Why do you think that?"
Client:	"Your receptionist just tried to sell me a cup of coffee."

***

The longer a document, the more likely it will be deleted from your computer.

"YOU KNOW, PART OF ME CAN'T WAIT TO GET BACK TO THE OFFICE. AT LEAST THERE I GET PAID TO STRESS OUT!"

Customer:	"I want to speak to an account representative."
Receptionist:	"If you call our 800 number and leave a message on the voice mail, someone will get back to you soon."
Customer:	"I have been leaving one message after another and no one calls back. I'm sick of machines. I want to talk to a competent, intelligent, warm-blooded human being."
Receptionist:	"I'm sorry, Maam, but we don't have any people like that working here."

* * *

Boss:	"Why are you quitting?"
Secretary:	"Because you promised me a steady job."
Boss:	"Well, isn't this a steady job?"
Secretary:	"No. Why there are two or three hours a night when I don't have anything to do but sleep."

* * *

> **In my case JOB is not a word but a very long sentence.**

You will be
paged the
moment you
sit down on the
toilet.

Office Epitaphs

Bookkeepers don't die, they go to their final audit.

Administrators don't die, they go to that big meeting in the sky.

Bosses don't die, they are delegated to the hereafter.

File clerks don't die, they are put into permanent storage.

Secretaries don't die, they put in eternal overtime.

Directors don't die, they issue their last annual report.

Managers don't die, they pass their final buck.

Typists don't die, they turn in their typing keys for keys to the Pearly Gates.

Copy clerks don't die, they go to the Xerox® of Ages.

Personnel directors don't die, they go to their final review day.

Supervisors don't die, they sign up for the eternal seminar.

Receptionists don't die, they greet their Maker.

Data processors don't die, they are systematically removed to the great beyond.

Computer programmers don't die, they byte the eternal bullet.

Switchboard operators don't die, they answer the big call.

Vice Presidents don't die, they climb their last corporate ladder.

Executives don't die, they go the big washroom in the sky.

Managers don't die, they take their last lap on the fast track of life.

Payroll clerks don't die, they are permanently withheld.

Messengers don't die, they make their last big delivery.

Programmers don't die, their disks are eternally erased.

Word processors don't die, they are permanently deleted from the archives of life.

Workers don't die, they are terminated by the Big Boss.

* * *

Secretary 1:   "Is your boss any fun?"

Secretary 2:   "Well if there is such thing as reincarnation, he will be back as a wet blanket."

* * *

Absence
makes
the boss
grow
madder.

Any day that
begins with
commuting
and ends
with
commuting
sucks.

**Actions speak
louder than
words; but a
well-written
memo can look
like you're
accomplishing
something.**

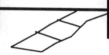

Boss:	"Last night I had the best, most tender steak I've ever had."
Secretary:	"Steak? Steak? Oh, yes, that's what I pass by on the way to the spaghetti section."

* * *

Boss:	"Why are you so mad?"
Secretary:	"Because we didn't get a bonus this year."
Boss (Handing her a roll of bills):	"Here. Now are you happy?"
Secretary:	"I could be happier."
Boss:	"All I have left is a bunch of change."
Secretary:	"I'm not picky."

* * *

Secretary 1:	"I'm getting a little nervous about my job."
Secretary 2:	"Why?"
Secretary 1:	"Well my boss says, 'Anything goes.'"
Secretary 2:	"Why does that scare you?"
Boss (calling from his office):	"Hey, Anything, come in here for a minute."
Secretary 1:	"Any more questions?"

* * *

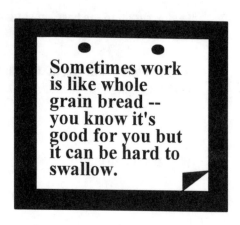

Sometimes work is like whole grain bread -- you know it's good for you but it can be hard to swallow.

Boss:	"Why are you quitting? Is your pay too low?"
Secretary:	"The pay is okay but I feel like I'm keeping a horse out of a job."

***

Manager:	"My secretary is suffering from the heartbreak of psoriasis and the pain of hemorrhoids."
Personnel Director:	"That's terrible. I didn't know she was sick."
Manager:	"She isn't. I dictated those words and she can't spell them."

***

Secretary 1:	"I complained to my boss that I was overworked here and at home and was burning the candle at both ends."
Secretary 2:	"Is he going to get you some help?"
Secretary 1:	"No. He's going to get me some more wax."

***

George:	"Why is your secretary jumping up and down at her desk doing cheers?"
Bill:	"She heard that her computer was down and is trying to cheer it up."

***

Secretary:	"I finally figured out why I never have enough money —you are cheating me."
Boss:	"How am I cheating you?"
Secretary:	"You pay me only for five days a week but I spend money seven days."

***

Secretary 1:	"What did you do all weekend?"
Secretary 2:	"I was getting ready for my mother-in-law's visit."
Secretary 1:	"Were you cleaning?"
Secretary 2:	"No, I was picking out the word "Welcome" from our front door mat."

***

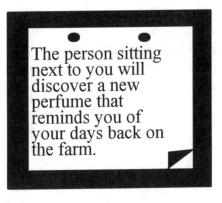

The person sitting next to you will discover a new perfume that reminds you of your days back on the farm.

Secretary 1:	"Is your boss's wife jealous of you?"
Secretary 2:	"No, she knows what I think of him."

* * *

Secretary:	"My boss is impossible to work for."
Personnel Manager:	"Why?"
Secretary:	"She's always early when I'm late and late when I'm early."

* * *

Secretary:	"My boss figures nothing is too good for me at Christmas, so that's what he gives me."

* * *

Secretary 1:	"I can't believe Miss Johnson is retiring. She doesn't look 65."
Secretary 2:	"Well, if you look under her make-up you'd believe it!"

* * *

Cindy:	"Does he cheat on his wife?"
Mindy:	"Well let's put it this way, if he was a bigamist and had 24 wives — he'd still have a mistress."

* * *

Jones:	"My wife is the secretary to the Archbishop but I don't think it's going to work out."
Smith:	"Why?"
Jones:	"They don't like her filing system."
Smith:	"What's wrong with it?"
Jones:	"She has two filing cabinets; one is marked sacred and the other is marked top sacred."

***

Boss:	"I'm a self-made man."
Secretary:	"You must have given the job to the lowest bidder."

***

Boss:	"Why didn't you remind me it was my wife's birthday?"
Secretary:	"That's not my job."
Boss:	"Well, now I'm in a big mess and I don't know how to get out of it."
Secretary:	"Now that's my job!"

***

**Hard work
never hurt
anyone else.**

"WELL THEN, CAN YOU TYPE *10* WORDS A MINUTE?"

Boss:	"Well, John did you understand all of that?"
John:	"Almost. I'm just not sure of the stuff between 'Dear Ms. Johnson' and 'Sincerely yours'."

***

Secretary 1:	"Why didn't you laugh at the boss's joke?"
Secretary 2:	"I don't have to — I'm quitting next week."

***

Boss:	"It's raining pretty hard out there, maybe you better stay until it lets up."
Secretary:	"Don't worry, Sir — it could never rain that hard!"

***

Secretary 1:	"My boss is really mad at me."
Secretary 2:	"Why?"
Secretary 1:	"I was an hour late and kept him waiting 10 minutes."

***

Secretary 1:	"Is your boss in?"
Secretary 2:	"Of course she's in. Do you think I'd look this busy if she wasn't?"

***

Secretary 1:	"Yesterday I told my boss he was a cheap SOB who should be shot."
Secretary 2:	"And he didn't fire you?"
Secretary 1:	"No, I hung up before he recognized my voice."

* * *

Secretary:	"I may have to quit. I'm working 60 hours a week and am about to collapse."
Personnel Director:	"Don't worry, all this pressure can't keep up forever. There's always a light at the end of the tunnel."
Secretary:	"In my case I think it's a search party looking for survivors."

* * *

Secretary 1:	"By the end of the day I'm really tired."
Secretary 2:	"Why?"
Secretary 1:	"My boss is a such a go-getter."
Secretary 2:	"So why are you tired?"
Secretary 1:	"All the time she tells me go get 'er this and go get 'er that."

* * *

Boss:	"Why do computers do more work than people?"
Secretary:	"They don't have to answer the phone."

* * *

Secretary 1:	"Why are you always at your boss's throat?"
Secretary 2:	"It's the furthest away from the area he wants me to kiss as I can get!"

***

Secretary 1:	"Are you ready for lunch?"
Secretary 2:	"I have to finish this letter before I leave."
Secretary 1:	"Did that SOB you work for tell you that?"
Secretary 2:	"No. In fact he just had a heart attack."
Secretary 1:	"That's terrible."
Secretary 2:	"Yes, I'm sending this letter asking the paramedics to come right away."

***

Secretary 1:	"I hear you're dating Joe from accounting."
Secretary 2:	"Yes I am."
Secretary 1:	"Do you think you two will get married?"
Secretary 2:	"I would never marry anyone who worked here — after all, they hired me!"

***

I couldn't start off the day on the right foot even if I was a centipede.

1.

"My wife's on her way up!"

2.

Secretary:	"I'm getting tired of you yelling at me to be more efficient all the time when you don't practice what you preach."
Boss:	"What do you mean? I have a daily work plan; I know where everything is; I am here early and stay late; I never waste time."
Secretary:	"Well, then why do you make me answer your phone when it's never for me?"

* * *

Secretary:	"I have to leave to catch my bus."
Boss:	"I thought you drove to work?"
Secretary:	"I did until last week."
Boss:	"Did your car break down?"
Secretary:	"No, I got such a great parking spot I hate to vacate it."

* * *

Behind every successful boss there's a secretary saying, "Like hell I'm going to stay late again."

* * *

If ignorance is bliss, then personnel should be the happiest place on earth.

In an office, familiarity breeds contempt -- and often a sexual harassment lawsuit.

Secretary 1:	"My boss is so generous."
Secretary 2:	"That's nice. What does he do?"
Secretary 1:	"Well, whenever I bring candy he shares his appetite."

***

Boss:	"Where have you been all morning?"
Secretary:	"I was in court having my name legally changed."
Boss:	"Why did you change your name?"
Secretary:	"To get a better parking space."
Boss:	"A better parking space? What did you change your name to?"
Secretary:	"Visitor."

***

A junior secretary in the accounting department pulled into the company parking lot, driving a brand new expensive sports car just as the secretary to the president was getting out of her rusty old car. Knowing that the secretary didn't make a lot of money she was curious how she could afford such a car.

"That's a great car," the executive secretary said, "but how can you afford such an extravagance?"

"Oh, I devised a new filing system for our department and that is how I came up with the money," the secretary beamed proudly.

"It must be a wonderful system. Did you get a bonus?"

"Oh no. In fact it is an awful system. We can never find anything."

"Well, just how did you get all that money from starting such a disjointed filing system?"

"Well, whenever anyone wants something I'm the only one who can find it. So I get a lot of overtime."

***

TYPING
(To the tune of "Wild Thing")

Next on Geraldo: Women Who Love To Type Too Much and the Men Who Buy Them Leather Copy Holders

Typing
You pull my heart strings,
I'm just a ding-a-ling, oh baby....
For Typing.

Typing
I think I love you,
But I want to know for sure,
So come on and let me stroke your keys
I love you.

Typing....
You make my bell ring,
I am your plaything — oh yeah,
Typing.

***

Boss: "You have a mind like a steel trap."

Secretary: "Well, thank you."

Boss: "Unfortunately I think the two hamsters you captured up there have died."

***

One day the power went out for a number of hours. Ms. Harrison became worried when she couldn't find her secretary Henry. When the power came back on Henry showed up at his desk.

"Where were you?" Ms. Harrison asked.

"I got stuck when the power went out," Henry replied, shaking his head.

"Oh no. Were you on the elevator?"

"No," Henry said, "the escalator."

***

Two secretaries were leaving a staff meeting that was chaired by an unpopular office manager.

"I just can't stand Mr. Washington," one said."

"I know what you mean," agreed the other. "As soon as he walked out the door everyone in the room was happy."

"I can think of one way everyone would have been even happier."

"How?"

"If he had walked out the window."

***

> Your doctor will finally call you back to discuss your gynecological problem when your boss is standing at your desk.

Boss:	"Did I hear you saying I have a thick head of hair?"
Secretary:	"I never mentioned your hair."

***

Sexual Harrassment

Brush-off:	The only way to touch anyone at work without getting a harassment claim filed against you.
Social security:	A Tic-Tac in every pocket.
Sexual harassment:	Gender bender.
Feminism:	The corporate "f" word.
Gender:	How you say "sex" without blushing.
Affair:	A business copulation complication.

***

Interviewer:	"Why are you looking for a new job?"
Applicant:	"I'm a victim of sexual harassment."
Interviewer:	"What do you do?"
Applicant:	"I'm self-employed."

***

"I UNDERSTAND YOU'RE LOOKING FOR A MAIL SECRETARY."

The boss
never looks
as old as he
or she is.

Dept. Manager:	"I think the president is a sex fanatic."
Personnel:	"Why do you say that?"
Dept. Manager:	"The only way he will read my memos is if I put them on a T-shirt and then dump a bucket of water on myself."

* * *

Secretary:	"I want to file a complaint about Mr. Jones."
Personnel:	"What's the problem?"
Secretary:	"He is too religious."
Personnel:	"Religious?"
Secretary:	"Yes, he wants to start each day with the laying on of hands."

* * *

| Secretary 1: | "Can I trust Paul?" |
| Secretary 2: | "Well I don't want to say anything bad but if he shakes your hand — you'd better count your fingers." |

* * *

Personnel Director:	"Miss Jones, you can no longer wear such tight clothing."
Miss Jones:	"Why?"
Personnel Director:	"None of the men can breathe."

* * *

| Personnel: | "Is it true you kissed Ms. Jones?" |
| Mr. Smith: | "No, and I'll never do it again." |

* * *

| Company President: | "Molly, I know we had an affair, but who told you that you could come to work when you pleased?" |
| Molly: | "My lawyer." |

* * *

Printers never jam when the service person is in the office.

The photo on your corporate ID badge will be even worse than the one on your driver's license.

Arnie:	"I hear you are retiring."
Marnie:	"Yep. I always said I'd retire as soon as I had half a million dollars to live on."
Arnie:	"You must have worked very hard and saved your money for years."
Marnie:	"No, my boss just made a pass at me."

***

The company president called the chief security guard into his office.

"Chuck, we have received a complaint from one of the employees that you are making obscene sexual comments and putting your hands where they don't belong. These unwanted advances will have to stop."

Chuck looked down at his feet and mumbled, "I'm sorry, Sir. I won't do it again."

The company president opened the door and said, "I'm sure Ms. Jones will be glad to hear that."

"Ms. Jones!" Chuck's face lit up, "I was afraid that Bob in Accounting had been complaining."

***

Chad:	"You know a lot of the chicks in the office say I'm God's gift to women."
Betty:	"That would explain why devil worshiping is on the agenda for our weekly staff meetings."

***

Personnel:	"Well, Charles, you made remarkable progress at this year's office party."
Charles:	"Thank you, Ms. Grant. I certainly am trying to be a more sensitive man and not offend any of the women in the office."
Personnel:	"We appreciate your efforts. Although next year we would appreciate your keeping your mouth and your fly closed."

***

Sales rep:	"I'd like to talk to your boss about buying encyclopedias for your firm library."
Receptionist:	"Oh don't waste your time — my boss already thinks he knows everything."

***

Your boss will introduce you to an important client when your mouth is full.

"WHAT DO YOU MEAN YOU'RE UNWINDING? YOU HAVEN'T EVEN BEEN TO WORK YET!"

Receptionist: "Would you like some coffee?"

Customer: "Yes, but no cream."

Receptionist: "I'm sorry we're out of cream, will you take it without milk?"

         * * *

Client: "I want to see someone around here with a little authority."

Receptionist: "Well, I have about as little as anyone. Can I help you?"

         * * *

Boss: "Why is Sally going to be late?"

Receptionist: "She says she has to have a tetanus shot before she can go back into your office."

         * * *

Client: "Is Mr. Jones in yet?"

Receptionist: "No, he's at the doctor's."

Client: "I hope he isn't sick."

Receptionist: "No. His secretary says he goes once a month to get a vaccine against charm."

         * * *

"MISS HOPKINS, WHEN I SAID TO 'PUT HIM ON HOLD' I ASSUMED HE WAS ON THE PHONE."

Boss:	"Why are you crying?"
Receptionist:	"I was just reading a very sad book."
Boss:	"A love story?"
Receptionist:	"No, my checkbook."

* * *

Receptionist:	"Bob had to go home to change his clothes."
Boss:	"Why?"
Receptionist:	"There was a sign in the lobby that said WET FLOOR so he did."

* * *

Boss:	"Good morning, how are you?"
Receptionist:	"I'm just fine."
Boss:	"Well, then, could you let your face know?"

* * *

Boss:	"Our receptionist is a translator."
Client:	"Oh really."
Boss:	"Yes, she can say 'Good morning' and it comes out 'Get the hell out of my face.'"

* * *

A church receptionist answered the phone, "Good morning, Rev. Jackson's office."

"Let me speak to that idiot right away," said the voice on the other end.

"I'm sorry, Sir," the receptionist replied, "but I can't possibly put you through to Rev. Jackson if you are going to speak that way. He is a man of God and deserves to be treated with respect. Now, who would you like to speak to?"

The voice on the other end replied even louder, "I want to speak to that stupid idiot, right now!"

"Sir," the receptionist said, "please try to refrain from using that language or I will have to hang up the phone."

The voice on the other end answered, "Listen here, lady, I have a million dollars I want to give to the church and..."

"Just a minute," the receptionist interrupted, "I see the stupid idiot coming down the hall now."

***

Vendor: "Is Mr. Jones in?"

Receptionist: "He's in a meeting and can't be disturbed."

Vendor: "But I have an appointment."

Receptionist: "Oh, well, then he was called out of the office on an emergency."

***

Receptionist: "Would you care for coffee while you wait?"

Client: "Yes — black, please."

Receptionist: "I'm afraid you'll have to take the same color as the rest of us."

***

"SOMEDAY, SON, THIS WILL BE ALL YOURS."

Manager: "Ms. Clark, I know we have a no-smoking policy in our office, but you have to learn to be more tactful with our clients. Mr. Garrison is a very important customer and was quite upset with how you treated him this morning after he lit a cigarette."

Ms. Clark: "I don't know why he's so mad. I stopped choking him when he put the cigarette out."

***

Customer: "Do you mind if I smoke?"

Receptionist: "I don't care if you spontaneously combust, just don't ask me to get you any coffee."

***

Getting up in the morning ruins my entire day.

Death on the job will not be tolerated.

Have A Nice Day

But don't flaunt it.

CURLY, FURRY, KIND OF WAVY, FAKEY LOOKING NEW TOUPEE

(To the tune of "Itsy, Bitsy, Teeny, Weeney, Yellow Polka Dot Bikini")

Dedicated to all those guys who believe they can recapture their youth by recapturing their hair.

She was afraid to go into his office,
She was afraid of what she would see,
She was afraid to go into his office,
She was as nervous as she could be.
  2-3-4 Tell the people what he wore.

It was a curly, furry, kind of wavy,
Fakey looking new toupee,
That he wore to the office today.
A curly, furry, kind of wavy,
Fakey looking new toupee
So at her desk she decided to stay.
  2-3-4 Stick around I'll tell you more.

She was afraid to go and get some coffee,
Because he might be at the machine,
She was afraid to go and get some coffee,
So she sat there and craved some caffeine.
  2-3-4 Tell the people what he wore.

It was a curly, furry, kind of wavy,
Fakey looking new toupee,
That he wore to the office today.
A curly, furry, kind of wavy,
Fakey looking new toupee
So at her desk she decided to stay.
  2-3-4 Stick around there's plenty more.

She was afraid to go down to the restroom,
On the way she might meet up with her boss,
She was afraid to go down to the restroom,
So she sat with her legs tightly crossed.
      2-3-4 Tell the people what he wore

It was a curly, furry, kind of wavy,
Fakey looking new toupee,
That he wore to the office today.
A curly, furry, kind of wavy,
Fakey looking new toupee.
So at her desk she decided to stay.

From her desk to the restroom,
From the restroom out the door,
Speeding home in her auto,
Guess there isn't anymore.

* * *

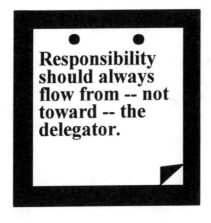

Responsibility should always flow from -- not toward -- the delegator.

Also available from Lincoln-Herndon Press:

*Grandpa's Rib-Ticklers and Knee-Slappers	$ 8.95
*Josh Billings -- America's Phunniest Phellow	$ 7.95
Davy Crockett -- Legendary Frontier Hero	$ 7.95
Cowboy Life on the Sidetrack	$ 7.95
A Treasury of Science Jokes	$ 8.95
The Great American Liar -- Tall Tales	$ 9.95
The Cowboy Humor of A.H. Lewis	$ 9.95
The Fat Mascot -- 22 Funny Baseball Stories and More	$ 7.95
A Treasury of Farm and Ranch Humor	$10.95
Mr. Dooley -- We Need Him Now! The Irish-American Humorist	$ 8.95
A Treasury of Military Humor	$10.95
Here's Charlie Weaver, Mamma and Mt. Idy	$ 9.95
A Treasury of Hunting and Fishing Humor	$10.95
A Treasury of Senior Humor	$10.95
A Treasury of Medical Humor	$10.95
A Treasury of Husband and Wife Humor	$10.95

A Treasury of Religious Humor	$10.95
A Treasury of Farm Women's Humor	$12.95
A Treasury of Office Humor	$10.95

*Available in hardback

The humor in these books will delight you, brighten your conversation, make your life more fun, and healthier, because "Laughter is the Best Medicine."

Order From:
> Lincoln-Herndon Press, Inc.
> 818 South Dirksen Parkway
> Springfield, Illinois 62703